BEYO
STATE

Labour markets, equalities
and human rights

Edited by Mick Carpenter, Stuart Speeden and
Belinda Freda

First published in Great Britain in 2007 by

The Policy Press
University of Bristol
Fourth Floor
Beacon House
Queen's Road
Bristol BS8 1QU
UK

Tel +44 (0)117 331 4054
Fax +44 (0)117 331 4093
e-mail tpp-info@bristol.ac.uk
www.policypress.org.uk

British Library Cataloguing in Publication Data
A catalogue record for this book is available from the British Library.

Library of Congress Cataloging-in-Publication Data
A catalog record for this book has been requested.

ISBN 978 86134 872 2 paperback
ISBN 978 1 86134 873 9 hardcover

Cover design by Qube Design Associates, Bristol.
Printed and bound in Great Britain by Henry Ling, Dorchester.

Contents

List of tables and figures

Tables

Figures

Notes on contributors

Anne Bellis is a research fellow at the Institute for Employment Studies She previously worked at the University of Sussex, as a researcher and lecturer in continuing education. Her doctorate was in 'race', language and culture in adult education and her research interests are: educational and labour market disadvantage and socially excluded groups, particularly refugees and minority ethnic communities. Recent publications (with others) include (2007) *Young mothers not in learning: A qualitative study of barriers and attitudes*, IES Report 439, Brighton: Institute for Employment Studies.

Teresa Cairns is an experienced adult educator and a life historian, and has worked for a variety of community organisations. As a research officer for the Learning from Experience Trust at Goldsmiths, she researched informal learning. She is now an independent consultant and researcher, with interests in community regeneration policy, informal and action learning, participatory approaches to evaluation, knowledge sharing and empowerment.

Mick Carpenter is Reader in Social Policy in the Department of Sociology, University of Warwick. He has researched and published widely in health and social policy and has evaluated community health, employment and regeneration projects in Coventry. His most recent publication is (2007) 'Gilding the ghetto again? Community development approaches to tackling health inequalities', in E. Dowler and N.J. Spencer (eds) *Challenging health inequalities: From Acheson to choosing health*, Bristol: The Policy Press.

Pamela Clayton is a research fellow in the Department of Adult and Continuing Education, University of Glasgow, and has a PhD in political sociology. She is the author of a variety of publications on vocational guidance especially targeted to those subject to the risk of social exclusion. Recent publications include: (2005) 'Blank slates or hidden treasure? Assessing and building on the experiential learning of migrant and refugee women in European countries', *International Journal of Lifelong Education*, vol 24, no 3.

Phil Cleaver is a postgraduate student and lecturer in the Department of Sociology at the University of Warwick, researching primary healthcare systems in the UK and Finland. He was a research associate for Coventry University's Community Research and Evaluation Service (CRES).

Belinda Freda worked as a project officer at the University of Surrey, researching issues such as refugee community group capacity building, voluntary repatriation, discrimination in the workplace and young people, discrimination and exclusion. She is currently a research support officer in the Research and Regional Development Division at the University of Sussex.

Colin Griffin worked for many years in the Department of Educational Studies, University of Surrey, where he is now a visiting senior fellow. He has published widely in adult education and lifelong learning, especially in the fields of curriculum and policy analysis. Among his more recent publications are: (2003) *Adult and continuing education: Major themes in education*, London: Routledge (5 volumes, joint editor with Peter Jarvis) and (2005) (joint author with David Gray and Tony Nasta) *Training to teach in further and adult education* (2nd edn), Cheltenham: Nelson Thornes.

Rhian McCarthy is Head of Bilingual Development at Coleg Llandrillo Cymru, Rhos-on-Sea, North Wales. Rhian has worked extensively in the field of adult education and her research interests include bilingualism, adult education and lifelong learning in rural areas. Publications include (with J. Scorrer) (2003) *Learning for community development in Wales*, Pontypridd: Glamorgan University.

Susan McGrath is a freelance researcher and consultant, working with the statutory and voluntary sectors. Her main expertise and interests cover working with disadvantaged communities, developing and maintaining functional networks, building individual and community confidence and validating life experience within the context of lifelong learning. Publications include studies of access to learning in rural communities and support networks of women returners to paid employment and learning. They include (2006) 'Promoting equality, engaging with diversity: a study of EU legislation shows the importance of listening to the communities under scrutiny', *Adults Learning*, vol 17, no 5.

Barbara Merrill is a Reader in the Centre for Lifelong Learning, University of Warwick. Her research interests are gender, class and adult education, citizenship, learning careers and identity, community-based learning and biographical approaches to research. Recent publications (with others) include (2007) *Using biographical and life history approaches in the study of adult and lifelong learning: European perspectives*, Frankfurt am Main: Peter Lang.

Brec'hed Piette is Head of the School of Lifelong Learning at the University of Wales, Bangor. Her research interests are in lifelong learning in rural areas, and in bilingual issues. She is currently director of an EQUAL 2 project that is looking at innovative ways of delivering lifelong learning to groups discriminated against in rural areas.

Azar Sheibani is Head of the Refugee Assessment and Guidance Unit (RAGU) based in the Department of Applied Social Sciences, London Metropolitan University. For the past 13 years she has worked in the refugee sector managing various projects at regional, national and transnational level. She previously worked as a researcher, and has three publications. She seeks to combine research on refugees and forced migration with practice in the same field.

Inga Šniukaité is a postgraduate research student and a part-time lecturer in the Department of Sociology, University of Warwick. Her doctoral research investigated feminist social action through the internet, examining cyberfeminism as an example of online social movements. She was a research associate at Coventry University's Community Research and Evaluation Service (CRES). Prior to her doctoral studies in the UK, Inga was involved in women's activism in Central Eastern Europe, both in non-governmental organisations and as a gender adviser in the Organization for Security and Co-operation in Europe's Mission in Kosovo.

Stuart Speeden is Reader in Public Policy and Head of the Centre for Local Policy Studies at Edge Hill University, Lancashire. He has worked extensively on equality in public services and is joint author of (2001) *The equality standard for local government*, London: The Employers' Organisation for Local Government. He is currently working on a new equality improvement framework for public services and on the management of values in public service organisations. Publications include (2006) 'Equality and regeneration: managing conflicting agendas for social inclusion', in J. Diamond et al (eds) *Managing the city*, London: Routledge.

Nick Walters was for many years a senior staff tutor and a researcher in the Department of Political, International and Policy Studies at the University of Surrey. His research includes many areas of social exclusion in British and European contexts. Publications include (2001) *Empowerment indicators: Combating social exclusion in Europe*, Bristol: The Policy Press.

Debby Watson is a research fellow at the Norah Fry Research Centre, University of Bristol. Her main research interests are around the inclusion of disabled children and adults in services and research, particularly those with learning and communication difficulties. Publications include (with others) (2004) *Making a difference? Exploring the impact of multi-agency working on disabled children with complex health care needs, their families and the professionals who support them*, Bristol: The Policy Press.

Claire Wickham is a senior disability officer in the Disability Resource Centre at the University of the West of England, Bristol. Her main research interests are around access to lifelong learning for disabled adults and the experience of D/deaf graduates in the labour market. The final report – *Disabled adult students and access to higher education: What I really, really want*, written by Jo Earl, Claire Wickham and Val Williams – is available at www.bristol.ac.uk/cacs/really-want-report.doc.

Val Williams is a senior research fellow in the Norah Fry Research Centre, University of Bristol. Her current research interests include supporting people with learning difficulties to take a full role in the research process. Recent projects include an inclusive study about personal assistance with the University of the West of England Centre for Inclusive Living. Her previous careers were in support services in further and adult education and in teaching. Her most recent publication is (with others) (2007) *A new kind of support*, Kidderminster: British Institute of Learning Disabilities (BILD).

ONE

Introduction: towards a better workfare state, or one beyond it?

Mick Carpenter, Stuart Speeden and Belinda Freda

Developing a bottom-up approach to evidence-based policy making

This book explores the ways in which it may be possible to shift away from the current trend in the UK towards a disciplinary 'workfare state'. It does so by first identifying the key messages arising from case study research by the eight UK universities involved in the SEQUAL Development Partnership into local case studies of inclusive, community-based approaches to accessing employment for people disadvantaged and excluded by reason of gender, class, ethnicity, disability, sexual orientation, language, geography, citizenship status, and youth and older age. As well as the specific policy and practice points that arise from the case studies, this evidence is generally seen as raising doubts about the work-first approach to employability dominant in the UK. The human capital approach associated with European social policy discourses is seen as more in tune with case study and wider evidence, and aligns more with the interests of people who are disadvantaged and discriminated against. The book, however, advocates an alternative capabilities and human rights approach as the most appropriate way forward beyond both employability and human capital approaches. In doing so, the book seeks to develop a bottom-up approach to evidence-based policy making, seeking to evaluate policies from the standpoint of those affected and targeted by them, utilising their experience and wisdom to open up broader policy debates (www.surrey.ac.uk/politics/cse/sequal.htm).

Background to the research and critique of dominant employability-based approaches

This book derives from the SEQUAL research funded under the European Union (EU) EQUAL Programme, which sought both to identify dynamics of disadvantage, and to identify promising practices aimed at overcoming barriers to labour market inclusion and progression. It was conducted in 2002-05 at a time when the UK was experiencing a sustained economic boom following recovery from deep recession in the early 1990s, leading to tight local labour markets in many areas. By this time, the main New Labour welfare-to-work reforms – the New Deals for Employment, tax credits, childcare subsidies and the National Minimum Wage (NMW) – had bedded in. However, despite these apparently favourable economic and policy circumstances, many people from the groups highlighted in the SEQUAL research were still experiencing difficulties in either gaining a foothold or sustaining their participation in a booming economy, and sharing in the spreading prosperity.

The SEQUAL research was funded under the 'employability' theme of the EU's EQUAL Programme for facilitating access or return to a labour market 'which must be open to all'. This provides a means for testing innovative and empowering approaches linked to the European Employment Strategy (EES) and social inclusion process, by promoting a more inclusive work life through fighting discrimination of the kind highlighted in the case study chapters (http://ec.europa. eu/employment_social/equal/index_en.cfm). To this end, it funds innovative initiatives through the European Social Fund (ESF) over a two- to three-year period, based on empowerment principles, to promote labour market inclusion and integration, on the assumption that the lessons will subsequently be widely 'mainstreamed'. It is important to realise in this regard that EQUAL is only a small cog within the larger mechanism of the EU's ambitious 2000 Lisbon Strategy to enable Europe by 2010:

> ... to become the most competitive and dynamic knowledge-based economy in the world, capable of sustainable economic growth with more and better jobs and greater social cohesion. (http://ec.europa.eu/employment_social/ employment_strategy/index_en.htm)

It therefore seeks to fuse the economic, social and environmental objectives together in three mutually reinforcing 'pillars'. Its economic pillar seeks to deepen the processes of economic liberalisation of the European Single Market, while the social pillar seeks to 'modernise the European social model by investing in human resources and combating social inclusion'. Both are linked to the EES, which is concerned to generate 'more and better jobs', with full employment by 2010 defined generally as a 70% employment rate, a female rate of 60% and a rate for workers over 55 of 50%. Progress on these and other measures is monitored through the so-called Open Method of Coordination against these and other agreed indicators (http://ec.europa.eu/growthandjobs/areas/fiche08_en.htm). The final key policy element, deriving from the 1997 Amsterdam Treaty, is a raft of measures to tackle labour market discrimination in the equalities areas addressed by the EQUAL Programme through the 2000 Framework Directives, on which the UK was required to legislate by 2007 (http://ec.europa.eu/employment_social/fundamental_rights/legis/lgdirect_en.htm).

On the face of it, UK domestic economic and social policies have many similarities with the Lisbon Strategy, which is not surprising given Britain's EU membership. These include efforts to modernise social policies and to tackle poverty and social exclusion by integrating people into paid employment, by the key welfare-to-work measures already identified, and promotion of a 'flexible' labour market. In addition, following the implementation of the Employment Directives, and the incorporation of the European Convention on Human Rights (ECHR) into domestic law through the 1998 Human Rights Act, the UK's anti-discrimination and equalities system is acknowledged to be the most developed in Europe. The new Equality and Human Rights Commission (EHRC) set up as a result of the 2006 Equality Act now oversees an integrated equalities system which, following the proposed introduction of a Single Equality Act, may enable forms of discrimination that occur together to be tackled together.

Although both are fundamentally grounded in neoliberal economic principles, there remain tensions between British and mainstream EU approaches, which have implications for the constraints and possibilities of community-based employment initiatives. Since Margaret Thatcher, and even before, Britain has had a more open and less interventionist economy, linked to the role of the City of London in the world economy (Gamble, 1994). The shift to flexible labour markets was facilitated by monetarist economic policies after 1979. While this did not fundamentally change with the election of New Labour in 1997, there were more supply-side employment initiatives and welfare-to-work measures at the national level, linked also to local experimentation of the kind focused on in this book. However, as we have seen, the EU's Lisbon Strategy gives greater priority to social objectives through enhancing skills, in order to promote economic growth through increased productivity, adopting in other words a human capital approach to improve the quality of jobs. While elements of this are found in the UK, its system more often prioritises early entry into existing employment, with progression expected to come later. It is therefore closer to the US 'work-first' approach, if a more state-centralised version of it.

In terms of the local impact of this system, the SEQUAL case study research into 'communities of interest' defined around forms of discrimination and economically disadvantaged 'communities of place' showed that economic prosperity and New Labour's supply-side social policies had enabled community-based initiatives (CBIs) to help some people to access the labour market. However, they were clearly starting to yield diminishing returns. The evidence and the voices coming from case studies indicated that further progress was being hampered by the wider policy framework within which initiatives were required to operate. As will be seen, the kinds of positive factors that enabled initiatives to make progress depended crucially on:

- local discretion to operate flexibly outside bureaucratic structures;
- a long-term trust relationship built up often over many years;
- a voluntary rather than a sanction-based relationship between project workers and service users in which power to act fundamentally rested with the latter.

It was frequently pointed out to us by project workers that the top-down, target-driven regime, informed by the short-term work-first approach focused on immediate employment, was hampering initiatives from making further progress. The most severely disadvantaged clients were often some distance from the labour market. The multiple personal barriers they experienced, often the result of accumulated structural disadvantage and discrimination in the past, were often greater than could be dealt with by short-term skills enhancement or motivational training (Dean, 2003). For those who could access the labour market, the advantages of the available insecure low-waged work compared to benefits were often marginal. In dealing with both these issues, initiatives were hampered by the fact that funding regimes often required them to place people in employment quickly, or risk losing contracts. They usually did not enable project workers to support their clients much, if at all, once they had secured employment. Project workers and users were also often acutely aware of the limits of supply-side approaches that required disadvantaged and discriminated-against people to integrate themselves within a daunting and often unjust labour market, where flexibility was more often required of workers than being offered by employers. Thus, it is possible to make an evidence-based case that both more intensive supply-side intervention *and* stronger demand-side intervention are required to tackle labour market disadvantage and discrimination.

This was occurring in a wider context that Peck (2001) has characterised as involving a shift to 'workfare states', which is occurring most rapidly in English-speaking countries such as the US, Australia and the UK, but is the new orthodoxy spreading across the developed world (Lødemel and Trickey, 2000; Hoefer and Midgley, 2006). Workfare was traditionally defined as compulsory work for benefits, classically the stone-breaking imposed under the Victorian Poor Law. However, it is increasingly defined as greater conditionality and 'labour activation' where, in return for benefits, claimants must demonstrate they are looking for work, participating in training, displaying the right motivational traits and taking up available jobs. Peck points to a key feature of workfare being growing individualisation associated with casework methods. This involves a contradictory mixture of external surveillance and sanctions, and encouragement to internal motivation and effort.

Underpinning this whole approach is a shift from sociological and structural explanations of unemployment and 'worklessness', emphasising the responsibilities of governments, to psychological or cultural explanations, emphasising individual responsibility and personal agency. These can tend to blame the victim by identifying 'welfare dependency' as the cause rather than symptom of labour market exclusion, thus requiring disciplinary 'welfare reform'. These explanations have been reinforced by the general fall in International Labour Organization (ILO) unemployment rates[1] since the 1990s and tight labour markets, and an influx of migrants willing to take jobs at prevailing pay rates.

Underlying the shift to workfare is a rational choice model that starts from a priori assumptions about people's situations, and how they (should) think and behave from an economic maximising point of view, rather than starting from their own values and life goals. Evaluation in this model then tends to be defined in the narrow and mechanical sense of 'what works' to ensure that people get jobs rather than what effects they have on improving their lives. There is much statistical evidence, but relatively little elaboration of the local realities experienced by people and interventions. The chapters in this book have therefore been written from a holistic evaluation perspective that looks at the interplay of structure and agency in shaping outcomes, defined from the standpoint of those for whom initiatives are expected to help. It therefore looks at how wider structures constrain people's agency, while giving due credit to how social policies and project effects may liberate it, consistent with 'realistic' evaluation principles (Pawson and Tilley, 1997; Carpenter and Merrill, 2007). We thus identify 'promising' rather than 'good' practices as there is much that also needs to be overcome in the wider environment if their potential is to be realised.

From Peck's analysis, it is clear that workfare is not completely 'repressive'. For example, using the language of empowerment (DWP, 2006) it seeks the active involvement of disadvantaged and excluded communities. Herein, however, lies a contradiction within New Labour, with efforts to square increasing external compulsion with the empowerment and approval of disadvantaged communities. Our evidence points to the conclusion that genuine empowerment can only come from freely exercised choice, and that this, together with more supply-side support and demand-side intervention, is the only realistic and socially just way of tackling labour market exclusion.

Thus, the book argues that the workfare or work-first approach is, for many, either inappropriate or counterproductive and is a breach of human rights principles. It suggests that human capital approaches to labour activation potentially have more humanistic and economic benefits, addressing productivity at the same time as addressing some of the inequalities faced by those at the base of the post-industrial service economy. As McQuaid and Lindsay (2005) argue, employability is a fairly recent term and is used in a range of narrower and wider ways. While a narrow approach is consistent with workfare, it can be defined in broader ways to take due account of wider contextual influences, such as wage levels and benefits traps, availability of childcare, transport, location of work, and employer policies, preferences and discrimination. This opens up a broader policy agenda, more in tune with a European emphasis on developing skills, combating discrimination and tackling inequalities. However, in our view it still primarily justifies action to address people's needs on economic grounds. There may indeed often be a strong economic or 'business' case for tackling disadvantage and promising equalities, calling into question New Labour's emphasis on 'work first'. However, even where it has an economic cost, we argue that a people-centred equalities approach is ethically justifiable on social justice grounds, which must expand people's freedom to either enter the labour market or pursue alternative valued goals. To this end, the book concludes by arguing for a broad-based capabilities and human rights approach as a third and more satisfactory evidence-based alternative to either work-first or human capital approaches (Ruxton and Karim, 2001).

Structure of the book

In working from evidence to policy conclusions, the chapters in Part One report on the messages and amplify the voices arising from the SEQUAL case study research into initiatives aimed at tackling diverse types of labour market exclusion. While a variety of methodological strategies were adopted, all worked closely with community partners and deployed naturalistic methods and qualitative evidence showing the *processes* by which community-based initiatives operated and the *realities* of the lives of people involved with them.

In Chapter Two on Coventry, Mick Carpenter, Barbara Merrill, Phil Cleaver and Inga Šniukaité examine the intersection of class, gender and ethnicity and the impact of labour market initiatives in a city that has undergone rapid structural change. Chapter Three, by Debby Watson, Val Williams and Claire Wickham, explores ways of linking the social model of disability to labour market issues, particularly focusing on the experiences of Deaf people. Stuart Speeden reports in Chapter Four on how voluntary and community organisations facilitate access to the labour market for minority ethnic women at high risk of exclusion. Chapter Five, by Brec'hed Piette and Rhian McCarthy, shows how geographical exclusion affects North West Wales, and reports on efforts to provide support to local people affected by it. In Chapter Six Anne Bellis with Teresa Cairns and Susan McGrath reports on the contrasting experiences of efforts to combat discrimination linked to sexual orientation in Brighton & Hove and Hastings, while Mick Carpenter and Belinda Freda in Chapter Seven investigate the efforts of a group of young people to make progress in a 'tough' labour market. In Chapter Eight Pamela Clayton reports on employability issues affecting older people in the Glasgow labour market, and Chapter Nine by Azar Sheibani focuses on the labour market experiences and perceptions of refugees in London.

Part Two then develops general policy implications from the case studies and other available evidence. Mick Carpenter with Stuart Speeden examines the origins and assesses the impact of New Labour's welfare-to-work policies in Chapter Ten. Then in Chapter Eleven Carpenter and Speeden with Colin Griffin and Nick Walters articulate the basis for developing an alternative capabilities and human rights approach in the context of the creation of the new EHRC, arguing that social class justice must be a concern alongside other equalities.

Note
[1] The internationally approved definition in terms of those seeking work, whether or not they are claiming benefits.

References

Carpenter, M. and Merrill, B. (2007) 'Qualitative and holistic evaluation of local labour market initiatives: a case study of Coventry', in I. Nicaise and P. O'Connell (eds) *Evaluating labour market programmes for groups at risk: Good practice and innovative approaches in research*, New Jersey/Amsterdam: Transaction/Spinhuis, pp 239-57.

Dean, H. (2003) 'Re-conceptualising welfare-to-work for people with multiple problems and needs', *Journal of Social Policy*, vol 32, no 3, pp 441-59 (http://eprints.lse.ac.uk/archive/00000338).

DWP (Department for Work and Pensions) (2006) *A new deal for welfare: Empowering people to work*, London: DWP.

Gamble, A. (1994) *Britain in decline: Economic policy, political strategy and the British state*, Basingstoke: Macmillan.

Hoefer, R. and Midgley, J. (eds) (2006) *International perspectives on welfare to work policy*, New York, NY: Haworth Press.

Lødemel, I. and Trickey, H. (eds) (2000) *'An offer you can't refuse': Workfare in international perspective*, Bristol: The Policy Press.

McQuaid, R. W. and Lindsay, C. (2005) 'The concept of employability', *Urban Studies*, vol 42, no 2, pp 197-219.

Pawson, R. and Tilley, N. (1997) *Realistic evaluation*, London: Sage Publications.

Peck, J. (2001) *Workfare states*, New York, NY: Guildford Press.

Ruxton, S. and Karim, R. (2001) *Beyond civil rights: Developing economic, social and cultural rights in the UK*, Oxford/London: Oxfam/Justice (www.oxfam.org.uk/what_we_do/resources/downloads/Civilrights.pdf).

Part One
Case studies in labour market discrimination and inequalities

Beyond the ghost town? The 'promising practices' of community-based initiatives in Coventry

Mick Carpenter, Barbara Merrill, Phil Cleaver and Inga Šniukaitė

Introduction: key themes

This chapter explores two major themes from a structure–agency perspective. First, it focuses centrally on how access to the labour market has been influenced by divisions and identities, through the case study of Coventry, a city that has undergone a rapid change from a manufacturing to a post-industrial city in the past two decades. Initially, the remit of the Warwick University SEQUAL research was to focus on class and gender, but given the multicultural character of the city, we added 'race' and ethnicity, and, in practice, could not ignore the messages in relation to age, health and disability that were coming through our research. We retain, however, a focus on class relations as a thread running through other divisions because they are now in danger of being overlooked. Neither European policy discourses nor anti-discrimination and human rights legislation see class discrimination as something to prohibit, issues that will be picked up again later, in Chapter Eleven. We have utilised a holistic approach through biographical methods that show how social divisions play out in the lives of real people, hopefully enabling us to follow C. Wright Mills (1959) and link 'biography and history'. While the structured shift to post-industrial capitalism is largley beyond local people's control, human agency can shape it in one of two ways. Individuals and collectivities can seek to challenge or alter the structures in which they operate or else they can seek to influence outcomes within them.

This connects to our second major theme, the transformative potential of community-based initiatives (CBIs) that have sought to pick up the human pieces following the periodic economic shocks in the city's history. We argue that on the whole Coventry's responses have recently been accommodative, in a period when Labour and the trade union movements experienced significant defeats under Thatcherism. This has, at national level, shaped the politics of New Labour, and is also reflected in the way that local initiatives work within the dominant employability discourse and welfare-to-work approach. However, this does prevent CBIs from making a real difference in enabling people to improve their situation in the labour market and lives in general. Additionally, the implications of what they do, and the way that they do it, could potentially provide a challenge to dominant policies. In looking at whether the initiatives have made a difference, we utilised qualitative evidence, drawing on the views of agency workers and unemployed users, and the criteria they thought important, rather than just focusing on official goals and targets. For space reasons in this chapter we primarily focus on the views and responses of unemployed users. Our approach departs from orthodox quantitative evaluation approaches that seek to provide 'objective' estimates on whether initiatives helped people into jobs. In our view, and developed in more detail elsewhere (see Carpenter and Merrill, 2006), this does not do justice to the complexity of causal processes, including project effects, and does not follow people long enough to assess whether getting a job actually improved people's lives.

Our working definition of CBIs are that they are outreach schemes based on voluntary participation aimed at enhancing the supply-side employability of disadvantaged people, sometimes linking to employers, operating outside the official structures of the job centre and agencies like Jobcentre Plus. Typically, they will be funded to do this through subcontracts from the employment service, and also through a bewildering variety of funding streams such as the European Social Fund (ESF), the Learning and Skills Council (LSC), New Deal for Communities (NDC) and the Neighbourhood Renewal Fund (NRF). We looked at a range of initiatives in the statutory (local government) and voluntary sector, but we did not look at the private commercial sector.

Our analysis starts with the broader structural context in Coventry, then moves to examine our selected initiatives and how they were perceived by the recipients themselves.

Beyond the ghost town: the changing Coventry economy

In 1953 a sociological text described Coventry as the 'most industrial city in Europe' and 'essentially a city of factory workers' (Kuper, 1953, p 31). This contrasts greatly with today as Coventry's labour market has now become more diversified. A typical worker is now more likely to work in a public service, education or a supermarket.

Coventry has undergone dramatic changes since the mid-1970s, with its economic base shifting increasingly from manufacturing to services. This has posed significant problems of social adjustment. The economic and political crises of the 1970s and early 1980s dealt a severe blow to the employment and prosperity of the city, and another recession in the early 1990s further accelerated the decline in manufacturing. Since the mid-1990s the city has experienced a substantial recovery, although manufacturing, as elsewhere in Britain, has continued to decline. Coventry is no longer the 'ghost town' of the famous Specials' song, but not everyone has benefited equally. The factory jobs that gave unskilled men of a previous era high-paid if alienated jobs have disappeared. Much of the expansion of the economy has been low-wage and 'flexible' retail employment. This has given rise to a 'divided city', as illustrated in Table 2.1. This details the multidimensional nature of labour market exclusion, the close linkages between spatial separation and social inequality, and the ensuing health and psychological damage occuring in its wake.

Overall, compared with other cities, Coventry has been modestly successful. According to the English Indices of Deprivation, Coventry ranked as 63rd worst out of 534 local authority areas in 2004, an improvement on 2000 when it ranked 50th worst. More significant, perhaps are the area-based differences, as inequalities appear to be widening between the 31 'priority' neighbourhoods and the remaining more affluent ones. There are also differences between 'deprived' priority areas with two inner-city areas (Hillfields and Foleshill) having a concentration of poor residents, many of whom are members of minority ethnic groups and new migrants, compared with predominantly white outlying social housing estates such as Canley and Willenhall.

A 2004 survey by Coventry University's Community Research and Evaluation Service (CRES) asked respondents not in work about the barriers that they had experienced in getting the type of work they wanted. Across the city, age – being too old or young – emerged as the most significant issue (29%), followed by childcare responsibilities and illness or disability, qualifications or lack of availability of jobs (CRES, 2005).

Table 2.1: Divided Coventry, 2004: illustrations on employment and related issues

	Priority neighbourhoods (%)	'Rest of city' (%)
In full-time paid work	40.4	46.6
In part-time paid work	12.0	14.4
Self-employed	1.3	4.7
Managerial and professional	13.0	24.0
Process, plant and machine operatives	14.4	8.1
Elementary occupations	20.4	9.5
No academic qualifications	53.8	38.7
Registered unemployed or seeking work	8.5	1.5
At home/not seeking work	16.0	10.6
Long-term sick or disabled	7.2	3.6
Working-age households with no one in paid work	26.5	14.4
Very satisfied with neighbourhood as place to live	17.5	32.4
Sense of a lot of choice and control over one's life	28.9	50.3
Worried about being able to make ends meet	22.4	10.6

Source: CRES (2005: Quality of Life Household Survey)

The transformative potential of community-based initiatives

"We're not the job centre": agency workers' ethics of care, empowerment and social justice

In exploring the effect that CBIs had in helping people either to cope better within unequal structures or to overcome the disadvantage, discrimination, subordination and oppression associated with them, we utilised a 'realist' framework drawn from Bhaskar (1993). Our argument is that at present the initiatives are largely, but not wholly, concerned with reproducing existing structures, but there are aspects of their approach that could have transformative effects if wider policy frameworks made it more possible.

The five major and two smaller initiatives we investigated were examples of a growing number that had largely emerged in the city since the mid-1990s. Some were voluntary, some public sector operating within the regeneration division of the city council. All sought to work in flexible and non-bureaucratic ways to engage disadvantaged people, particularly those defined as 'hard-to-reach', and to provide intensive support, often of an individualised kind, to acquire or enhance personal, social and substantive skills, encouraging and assisting job search, and fostering integration in the local labour market. However, voluntarism was seen as a key element to an empowering approach that allowed 'clients'[1] to decide what was in their best interests. This was a value commitment, but was also seen as a marketing necessity, as reputation and word of mouth were often seen as the best methods of recruitment. Significantly, one of the key means by which the initiatives promoted themselves to unemployed or economically inactive people was that, as agency workers repeatedly said, "We're not the job centre".

The aim was to identify and address a range of issues that might be affecting people's access to the labour market, but also the general quality of their life. Confidence building often formed a core area of work. Agency workers sought to identify a wide range of issues such as health, childcare or debt, which could, if addressed, improve employability and address a person's needs. Although providing access to employment was seen as central, they claimed to have a general commitment to addressing whatever problematic issues arose.

Despite this common 'core' approach, there was considerable diversity in the initiatives. Some, like the general and mental health employment projects, were specific projects financed by an NRF or the ESF as in the case of the two Canley projects and the Community-based Economic Development (CBED) project. Others were the Client Support and Research Unit (CSRU) in the public sector, with a spread of funds, and the voluntary-based Willenhall Education, Employment and Training Centre (WEETC), Working Actively to Change Hillfields (WATCH) and Foleshill Women's Training (FWT). The voluntary organisations were closely linked to their disadvantaged locality, but did not always restrict their activities to it. The Muslim Resource Centre (MRC) was based in Foleshill but had a citywide remit. Although voluntary organisations had some time-limited core funding, most, if not all, of the employment-related activities were governed by conditional contracts. Some, for example, were required to deliver qualifications for the LSC, and place people in jobs within 13 weeks for the job centre, sometimes having to meet contrasting targets for the same group of clients. The initiatives, therefore, while having some discretion in how they accessed 'hard-to-reach' local people, were in most instances required to meet quantitative targets.

The voluntaristic principle was seen as key to empowering people to get jobs:

> 'There is never any pressure on anybody to do anything they don't want to do. It is giving the choice.... Because it's opening up opportunities, it's giving people the choice to you know if they want to take part in something.' (Female employment worker, Canley)

A holistic approach to clients was characteristic among agency workers, who viewed personal and social benefits, for example, as being just as important as getting people into jobs. The full project report argues that the biographies, perspectives and associated commitment of agency workers had positive influences on the delivery of the programmes (Aleksandraviciene et al, 2005).

Disrupted biographies and unemployed journeys

We undertook 50 tape-recorded interviews with unemployed users of CBIs that were transcribed and analysed using NVivo. We were interested in their individual narratives or employment and unemployment 'journeys', and how these connected to broader transformations in the city, linking 'biography and history'. There is only space here, however, to give brief portraits of these complex and multifaceted lives.

The men in our study generally tended to have some experiences in common. One of these, whether they had qualifications or not, was an unhappy time at school, and another was strong emotions about their experiences: "Like I say, I was anti-establishment from about nine years old. I hated school ... teachers used to hate me" (Dave,[2] age 36, WATCH).

Dave had a 'fractured' biography that cast a long shadow over his life, having been in the care of social services from the age of 11 to 18, and he had had a disrupted employment record. He contrasts this with his brother's better fortune in the labour market, who was able to ride the crest of the wave of the new post-industrial finance. Dave had done door work, had got into drugs, and had had spells of homelessness. His brother's success, despite a similar background, heightened Dave's sense of personal failure.

Curtis (age 36, WATCH), a second-generation African-Caribbean man, with parents in employment, left school without any formal qualifications. He preferred not to talk about it, focusing more on his City and Guilds Levels 1 and 2 in painting and decorating. He had had experience of a number of employment schemes having previously done landscape gardening as part of the 'Community Programme'.

By contrast, those asylum seekers and refugees we interviewed were often highly qualified: "I was student in Afghanistan. And this time started … started like revolution in 1978, yeah. The government sent me in Russia for high education…. I finished that education in 1986. Got my master's degree in history" (Nasser, age 49, WEETC).

A number of the middle-aged men who had grown up in Coventry had experienced spells of unemployment during their lives, having been made redundant several times. Bill had been at Leyland cars, then in the 1980s shifted to GEC (an electric goods manufacturer), but that ended after a couple of years:

> 'Oh yes I have had windows of unemployment. During those times I have either been out short term or longer period of times when I have been doing some work training to get my skills updated.' (Bill, age 58, WEETC)

These cases show how a combination of personal troubles linked with a vulnerable social position as age, health, ethnicity, local economic change and distant politics disrupt some men's lives and their participation in the labour market. Some men connected these elements together:

> 'I had worked at various major manufacturers in Coventry until 1991 when I was at the Jaguar [plant] and was made redundant. Since then I have not managed to gain proper employment. Yes, I was made redundant with 7,500 others. Well, the week I was made redundant, this city lost 28,000 engineering jobs. 28,000 went and Courtaulds closed and factories closed – it was the proverbial ghost town. (Bernard, age 53, WATCH)

There were other examples of how individual biographies and the wider narrative of the shift from industrialism to post-industrialism intersected. For example, an older Pakistani man, a client of the MRC, had worked for Courtaulds before it closed down and had not worked since; he was then in receipt of Incapacity Benefit as a result of long-term depression and anxiety.

One way of understanding these experiences is via Bury's (1988) concept of 'biographical disruption', devised to account for the impact of disability on people's lives. This applied directly to some of the men in our study. For example, Michael, a second-generation African-Caribbean man (age 35, WATCH), had been the victim of a serious car accident. He was in hospital for two years and had spent the past eight years on Incapacity Benefit. We think that the concept also has wider applicability. For many of the older men, despite some previous tendencies to instability, unemployment disrupted their expected male lifetime career pathway. For the younger men, the difficulty was in gaining a foothold in the labour market. For refugees and asylum seekers, political events disrupted their biographies. There was no sign among the men we interviewed of a 'culture of worklessness' where unemployment was 'normal'. Rather, the various circumstances that they experienced made it difficult to construct a male employment biography.

For the women, patriarchal structures and attitudes did not necessarily make unemployment or economic inactivity 'biographically disruptive'. On the whole the female clients in our study were younger than the men. One common theme among the diverse group of women we interviewed was a lack of confidence in their own abilities. Debby had had a fragmented employment career working in a string of low-paid supermarket or equivalent jobs, had two children and lived on a run-down housing estate known locally as 'doss city'. Conforming to a more widespread pattern, she did well educationally up to her teenage years, gaining 10 GCSEs, but failed to get any 'A' levels:

> 'Got into boys, unfortunately. I didn't revise as much as I should. I did take Sociology and English Literature and then I left school.' (Debby, age 28, WEETC)

Other white women had established an employment career from disadvantaged class backgrounds, seeking to advance in traditional and expanding female areas such as nursing, catering and clerical work. Jenny went to college and got more 'O' levels, and did a pre-nursing course:

> '... and then I went on to do my SEN [state-enrolled nurse] training and passed that, but then I left to have the children and have never gone back.' (Jenny, age 45, WEETC)

Subsequently Jenny re-entered the labour market full time and worked her way up to being supervisor and head cook in a canteen. Since her husband is profoundly deaf, they had taken the decision that she would be the main breadwinner. At the time of the interview she was exploring the possibility of taking a refresher course to re-enter nursing as a career.

Another white woman was well qualified, but had experienced the effects of a life where others made decisions for her. She left school "before I finished my exams" to go into banking:

> 'It was my mum saying "go on that will be a good job" ...
> she didn't even give me time to really think about what I
> wanted to do.' (Marie, age 42, WEETC)

Then marriage and children came along. The husband was "yes, very old-fashioned ... he didn't want me to work, the family didn't". She heard about the local bank needing someone "desperately" and got back in; she then had a varied career in banking, but this was disrupted by a serious back injury. At the time of the interview, Marie was in receipt of Incapacity Benefit, had divorced her husband and was sharing custody of the children. The sense of a life lived largely according to other people's requirements also came across in Joan's account (age 48, CSRU), an African-Caribbean woman who had had a succession of low-paid jobs constructed around children and her husband's shift work. As a result of family tensions she had found it increasingly difficult to combine the two. She decided after her father's death that she 'needed a break' to create some autonomy for herself, and had not worked for the two years prior to our interview.

For Asian women, marriage and children often formed the primary basis of their lives (see also Chapter Four). For those from more traditional backgrounds, the idea of *having* to work seemed undesirable and even demeaning for a married woman. However, a number of Asian women we spoke to had become disillusioned when the reality did not live up to expectations, like Shirin, a Muslim woman born in the UK who had endured abuse from her husband and discovered that he had another wife and two children:

> 'I wanted children, he wouldn't let me have children. That
> was the turning point. That's when I decided to get out
> and start doing something for myself.... He wouldn't let
> me work and he wouldn't let me go out, only to go my
> parent's house.' (Shirin, age 36, FWT)

She separated from her husband despite the stigma in the community attached to divorce and separation. The interviews with Asian women showed considerable diversity, depending on age and generation. Some of the older women had worked in Coventry's industrial economy. First-generation Asian women mentioned the educational and language barriers they faced.

The negotiation of a dual identity or biography as a worker and as a mother/wife came across in many of the narratives, mediated by culture and material circumstances. In many cases, women had ultimately made real choices within strongly constrained structures, and, as in the case of Joan, and some of the Asian women interviewed, this can involve rejection of an employment identity. However, rather than see these decisions as 'preferences' or lifestyle choices, as the work of Hakim (2005) suggests, the women we interviewed were often hemmed in by poverty, ill health, community proscriptions and patriarchal impositions. Against these they therefore had to struggle to make choices and realise their 'capabilities', in Sen's (1999) sense. Additionally, Hakim's notions of classifying women according to their orientation to the labour market and child-bearing does not seem to fully take account of the twists and turns that are revealed by our narrative accounts.

Client perceptions of Coventry community-based initiatives

Many men heard about the initiatives from friends, had dropped in, or responded to newspaper advertisements. Asylum seekers and refugees in particular accessed agencies through their community networks. Overall, there was strong criticism of official employment services. Thus Mohammed (age 32, WATCH) was not alone in contrasting the CBI with the job centre:

> 'Because I was going to the job centre but I wasn't getting anything. Even, er, I am talking six or seven years ago and even now when I go down there, I get nothing. I don't know, someone told me about the WATCH centre and I thought I would go and look them up and get my CV made up and something like that.'

This was a recurrent theme. The recent shift in Jobcentre Plus towards a 'self-service' model had not pleased everyone:

'Yes, that's all the job centre is, that's what it's all about – it's actually a way of regulating the labour market, yes keeping the wages down.' (Bernard, age 53, WATCH)

Also:

'Okay everybody has got the attitude, oh it can be done with computers, you don't need client contact….You used to have the instant rapport with a physical person….You know they can test out far better in person than over the phone…. Because the job centre staff are set a target of so many people to get jobs and so many people into permanent employment a day.' (Bill, age 39, CSRU)

Younger clients similarly criticised Connexions, the youth employment service. One young man felt that they were concerned primarily with getting "bums on seats" to meet their targets. The men interviewed variously found the official employment services distant, uninvolved, lacking time, concerned with government targets or with "hidden agendas", that they were not in the clients' interest as "they administer the unemployed".

This contrasted with their experience of CBIs, which were felt to be accessible, gave them time and attention, "treating us as people" and "more than a number" or someone to be pressured into taking a job. Often it was the range of practical services offered that was appreciated, such as developing a CV, filling in forms, assisting in job search and interview techniques. It was also clear that the close relationships established with staff made a significant difference. Regular and patterned contact with the initiative provided 'structure' and social engagement that helped to turn lives around. A substantial number of the men had engaged in voluntary work as a means of socially engaging and enhancing their skills. One consequence was that their communities had respectively become dependent on this, involving a potential loss should they get jobs. This supports arguments that more efforts should be made to recognise the validity of unpaid community work by more flexible benefits, regulations and the provision of pathways into the social economy through intermediate labour markets and similar schemes. A range of outcomes needs to be seen as valid, not just qualifications and job placement numbers. This is taken up in the discussion of policy alternatives in Chapter Eleven.

Rather than producing sudden change, the CBIs were slowly building or rebuilding confidence, skills, improving health and dealing with debt. Several male clients talked about the benefits of establishing a long-running relationship with agencies, hoping that this would enable them to get low-paid jobs initially but in the longer run to move up the jobs ladder. There are legitimate concerns that this might lead to long-term dependency through 'churning' and project tourism. The biographies also revealed that a sizeable number of the men interviewed had multiple problems, making it difficult to access the labour market in the short term. This dovetails with findings from other qualitative research, for example, by Dean et al (2003), and has implications for welfare-to-work policies and funding regimes that primarily assume that clients are virtually 'job ready', explored further later in Chapters Ten and Eleven.

There were some muted criticisms. For example, some older men who had been skilled workers in the 'old' Coventry economy thought the initiatives were primarily aimed at enabling people to secure low-paid 'first-rung' positions in Coventry's 'new' economy rather than providing the means by which they could acquire positions equivalent to those they had lost. Some of the younger clients felt that the training and services were too general, and they wanted specific training such as in forklift truck driving, heavy goods vehicle (HGV) training, and health and safety and hygiene. Project workers were aware of some of these issues.

Women's experience of initiatives sometimes also drew negative comparisons with the job centre. Additionally, whereas the white men seem to have in many instances 'stumbled' on an initiative, white female clients in the study seemed to have more often sought it out. For example, as Brenda (age 36), a participant in the New Opportunities for Women (NOW/CSRU) programme, put it:

> 'By then I was 36 and thinking oh gosh what am I going to be, you know, what can I do now. What schemes can I get on. Actually in the January I did see there was a big write-up in the paper about this course for women.'

She went along to CSRU as a result of her mandatory job centre review, where she received the leaflet and eventually signed up for the course, and at the time of the interview stated "I am really loving it". For her it offered practical skills and "it wasn't about pushing you into a job regardless of your wishes".

The NOW programme sought to pick up issues through counselling to deal with debt and personal relationships and provided assertiveness training to build confidence. One of the most important features of

NOW's approach was in helping women to identify the skills they already had, including the practical, social and interpersonal skills they had acquired through their informal family or community work. In contrast, initiatives helped men to learn new skills to make them 'fit' for the new economy, while CBIs sought to build women's confidence by showing them that they already had substantial grounding in such skills. Like the men, the quality of the relationship with staff was important. As Nasreen (age 31, CSRU) put it, "they're very kind, very nice people".

The Asian women accessed FWT most often through word of mouth. For the most disadvantaged women, cultural barriers existed to participating in training schemes in the public sphere. FWT was seeking to overcome this by walking a balancing act of trying to empower women at the same time as being 'sensitive' to community values, as also discussed later, in Chapter Four. Traditional Asian men were reassured, it was claimed, by the fact that it was a community-based women-only organisation.

Conclusion: the transformative potential of promising practices or enforced integration into 'poor work'?

These were small-scale case studies in one city and we are therefore cautious about drawing generalisations, especially as we talked to those accessing CBIs, not those who may have voted with their feet. However, it was clear that such initiatives were appreciated by those we interviewed, supporting the claims made by agency workers. There were many small ways in which it seemed apparent that they were helping to transform the lives of the people who came into contact with them. First, they were operating in holistic ways by addressing the broader needs of clients, rather than focusing only on equipping them for the labour market. Second, although qualifications and employment were part of meeting targets, they did not in either agency workers' or clients' eyes seem to define the scope of what was done. Employment was seen as a positive outcome for many, but not necessarily all. Third, the way that they were operating seemed a major reason for the successes made. This derived from the clear values of combined ethics of care, empowerment and social justice (eg, contrary to the argument of Gilligan (1982)), as well as simply providing time for people and "being nice", as one of the clients put it. This was partly linked to the 'feminine' culture of initiatives, but fundamentally it derived from 'thoughtful commitment' that combined humanistic values and planned 'goal-oriented' strategies.

The limitations of initiatives, often identified by agency workers themselves, were the need to work within a supply-side system that:

- expected quick results, and did not sanction longer routes to employment;
- provided little possibility for support once what was defined as 'sustainable' employment was achieved;
- operated an 'all or nothing' benefits system that expected unemployed people to risk the relative security of benefits for insecure employment and limited material advantages.

Project workers and sometimes their clients were also aware of the structural effects of class, gender, age, 'race' and disability. In many accounts of clients and agency workers, the impact of a global economy, and of a state that through its employment services was seeking to compel people into work, were seen as negative influences, along with the discriminatory practices of employers. If initiatives are to have broader transformative effects, then these demand-side issues must also be tackled, and the limits of personal agency acknowledged.

We believe that our approach, comparing and contrasting the views of project workers and clients, and exploring the role of structure and agency through biographical methods, illustrates some of the complexities involved and how a balanced and differentiated set of policy responses might be more appropriate. Giving space to the voices of clients and agency workers generates insights for devising a better system.

As well as what initiatives were doing, the way that they were doing it provides the key to why they seem to be more appreciated than mainstream services. The social relationships involved are fundamentally supportive but democratic, encouraging but respectful of people's choices, focused on employment but taking account of wider issues and needs. These could provide the germ for a reformed welfare-to-work system, which could work in complementary ways to existing employment services. The danger of shifting provision to CBIs, as appears to be increasingly mooted, is that if it is not done with care, it could undermine their positive features and particularly their democratic and flexible relationships, reproducing the bureaucratic and target-driven rigidities of mainstream services. However, an opportunity does exist for a more phased delegation of responsibilities to local communities, so long as not all the responsibilities are dumped on them and the government takes greater demand-side responsibilities.

Thus, what is promising about the practices we have examined cannot be isolated from the way they have done it. What constrains rather than enables initiatives is the broader policy and funding contexts in which they operate, and particularly government attempts to solve the problem of poverty and 'worklessness' primarily by integrating people into paid work rather than tackling structural inequality. There is therefore a parallel need, alongside a shift to a 'new localism', to improve the quality of base-level jobs rather than just finding better ways of cajoling people into them.

Notes

[1] We use this as the discourse most often used by agency workers, signalling a focus on the individual and the voluntary, service-focused character of the encounters.

[2] All names are fictitious.

References

Aleksandraviciene, I., Carpenter, M., Cleaver, P., Hussain, Z., Jovanovic, J. and Merrill, B. (2005) *More than a number: The impact of community-based initiatives on unemployed men and women in Coventry*, Guildford: SEQUAL Development Partnership, University of Surrey.

Bhaskar, R. (1993) *Dialectic: The pulse of freedom*, London: Verso.

Bury, M. (1988) *Living with chronic illness: The experience of patients and their families*, London: Unwin Hyman.

Carpenter, M. and Merrill, B. (2006) 'Qualitative and holistic evaluation of local labour market initiatives: a case study of Coventry', in I. Nicaise and P. O'Connell (eds) *Evaluating labour market programmes for groups at risk: Good practice and innovative approaches in research*, New Jersey/Amsterdam: Transaction/Spinhuis, pp 239-57.

CRES (Community Research and Evaluation Service) (2005) *Household surveys and community profiles*, Coventry: CRES.

Dean, H., MacNeill, V. and Melrose, M. (2003) 'Ready to work?: understanding the experiences of people with multiple problems and needs', *Benefits*, vol 11, no 1, pp 19-25.

Gilligan, C. (1982) *In a different voice: Psychological theory and women's development*, Cambridge, MA: Harvard University Press.

Hakim, C. (2005) 'Sex differences in work-life balance goals', in D.M. Houston (ed) *Work-life balance in the 21st century*, Houndmills, Basingstoke: Palgrave Macmillan, pp 55-79.

Kuper, L. (ed) (1953) *Living in towns*, London: Crescent Press.

Mills, C.W. (1959) *The sociological imagination*, New York, NY: Oxford University Press.

Sen, A. (1999) *Development as freedom*, Oxford: Oxford University Press.

THREE

"It's about having a life, isn't it?": employability, discrimination and disabled people

Debby Watson, Val Williams and Claire Wickham

Introduction

This chapter discusses access to employment for those deemed 'disabled'. Lessons learnt from the situation of Deaf[1] and disabled people raise questions about how best to achieve an inclusive employment sector, and therefore have general implications for employment policy. The issues for Deaf and disabled people also lead to questions about the nature of 'work', empowerment and participation, and about ways of creating greater flexibility and job satisfaction. Work and employment are all part of "having a life", as one disabled person put it, which is relevant for anyone, disabled or non-disabled.

The starting point for this chapter is that Deaf and disabled people have a right to define themselves and articulate their needs, and over the past 20 years they have increasingly come to define themselves as 'disabled by barriers in society'. This 'social model' of disability shifts the focus for responding to impairment from 'fixing' individuals to changing the wider society and the way in which it relates to disabled people, as well as to the Deaf community (Oliver, 1990). With this in mind, the chapter starts by considering the issues of unemployment and underemployment for disabled people, reasons for the 'employment paradox' and the insufficiency of recent policy and practice initiatives. While a 'disabled' identity seems to dominate labour market experiences, Deaf and disabled individuals have a range of identities on which they draw. In the light of these issues, the central part of the chapter presents findings from the Bristol SEQUAL research, which worked with Deaf and disabled people to identify barriers to employment and potential solutions. We then consider the societal-level policies and practices that may help to overcome structural barriers to the employment of

Deaf and disabled people, and finally summarise key messages and recommendations.

The employment paradox for disabled people

At the time of the research the employment rate for disabled people in Britain in 2004 was 51% compared with 81% of the non-disabled population. More than one million unemployed disabled people wanted a paid job (DWP, 2002). The numbers of people claiming Incapacity Benefit have risen since the early 1990s, while numbers of other claimants have fallen, in a generally buoyant labour market. As Stanley (2005) points out, in 2003, 8.7% of the working-age population claimed benefits as a result of sickness or disability. The major reasons for this growth were the more severe employment problems in areas hit by deindustrialisation, and tacit official encouragement for people to move onto the higher rate Incapacity Benefit in order to help reduce the unemployment count. Belatedly, the government has then sought through 'welfare reform' to rein in a 'problem' largely of its own creation, incidentally providing a neat illustration of how politics and economics can shape disabled identities.

Recent policy analysts have puzzled over the seeming inability of employment policy and support initiatives to reverse these trends. For instance, Roulstone and Barnes (2005) discuss whether policies such as the New Deal for Disabled People (NDDP) are themselves basically sound, but have faults in implementation. They identify many potential factors preventing successful implementation, such as benefit traps and prevailing labour market conditions. They also argue that government job targets often result in a focus on those who are almost 'job ready', to the exclusion of other disabled people. This is echoed for other groups in a number of chapters in this book, and its general implications are assessed in Chapter Ten later. However, for Roulstone and Barnes (2005, p 1) the fundamental issue is that 'disability and employment policy is premised on an inappropriate model of disability', based firmly within a medical model, with the onus on the individual disabled person to fit into an unchanging and often hostile work environment. According to Warren (2005), government policies have only started to tinker with this system through strategies that focus on pressurising the individual disabled person to 'improve' their employability in order to access employment, but do not go beyond 'the factory gate' to bring about the fundamental changes needed in the employment sector.

The social model of disability therefore provides a powerful impetus towards alternative visions of inclusive employment. Since the 1980s, the disability rights movement has become an important political force (Campbell and Oliver, 1996). Like other oppressed groups, disabled people have mobilised collectively and challenged dominant definitions of disability in terms of medically defined deficits of one kind or another, and pointed to the need to address 'social and political change' (Oliver, 2004, p 9). Physical and social barriers derive from the ways in which assumptions of 'non-disabled' normality are institutionalised in social life. In the field of employment, for instance, it is taken for granted that people will be able to read job adverts, transport themselves to work, and communicate through speech with other employees. These features of the employment scene are so common that they have become almost 'invisible' to employers, advisers and policy makers. The continuing dominance of the medical over the social model is also reflected in research that still focuses mainly on 'supply-side' measures, to improve the employability of disabled individuals, rather than 'demand-side' measures, which would focus on changing environments (Piggott et al, 2005).

A social model, however, will help us to recognise the barriers to successful employment that are embedded in the system. In order to include Deaf and disabled people in employment, the system itself will need to adapt to the needs of a diverse workforce. The 1995 Disability Rights Act as amended in 2005 goes some way in this direction; however, it remains set in a predominantly individualistic framework, with the requirement only to make 'reasonable adjustments', and arguably prioritises employers' needs over disabled people's rights.

The Bristol SEQUAL research and findings

The Bristol-based research (2003-05) worked collaboratively with disabled people to profile the employment situation in South West England, identifying the main disabling barriers and promising practices that overcame them. As far as practicable the project sought to provide employment opportunities to disabled people. It was supported throughout by a group of Deaf and disabled consultants with a range of impairments, some representing organisations of disabled people. Five meetings were held during the project, and three of the consultants carried out paid work for it. The research reviewed issues for people with learning difficulties, and Deaf/disabled people. It also conducted a general literature review and mapped local employment initiatives to support disabled people into work, the latter being the main focus of this chapter. The work, carried out in conjunction with the Deaf and disabled consultants and their contacts, utilised an existing employment network, a local council guide and contacts with disabled people's organisations. A postal survey in three areas (a large city, a semi-rural area adjoining a city and a large rural county) identified 27 initiatives where managers were interviewed, and a further 11 initiatives where they provided questionnaire information.

Two focus groups with disabled people were conducted and there was extensive consultation with the disabled consultants. The aim was to discover whether the views of disabled people matched the claims made by employment initiatives and, where there were discrepancies, we were led by the voices of disabled people. The executive summary from the research was made available to all participants and was also produced in an 'easy read' format. A 'Plain Facts' (www.bris.ac.uk/Depts/NorahFry/PlainFacts/NewPlainFacts/html/pfs/pf45.html) version of the findings, relevant to people with learning difficulties, was produced, using pictures and short simple sentences. One of the disabled consultants went on to chair our major mainstreaming event and another has been a co-author for a peer-reviewed article, thus, we hope, enhancing their future employment possibilities.

When including the voices of Deaf and disabled people, and service users generally, there are always issues of representation and perspective. There is now a considerable literature on the rationale and methodology for conducting emancipatory or participatory research (Zarb, 1992; Oliver, 1997; Beresford, 2003). As Oliver (1997) points out, emancipatory research is about the control and power exerted by disabled people, through their own organisations. The current SEQUAL project did not meet these standards, but the disabled consultants to the project had considerable experience in the disabled people's movement, including disability employment issues. During the course of the research, it became clear that there were significant differences between messages that rely on individual experience, and those that reflect a more 'politicised' stance. People will always bring to the research process their own life histories, issues and experiences. The issues that they raise are then at an individual level, against the backdrop of a societal structure that is not questioned. However, through the course of discussions, and actually carrying out the research, they become exposed to a wider range of perspectives and will seek to identify barriers and solutions at the societal level. We therefore present the findings about employment barriers below under these two headings – individual and societal.

Barriers identified by individual experience

The participants in the focus groups and our disabled consultants stated that 'internal' barriers played some part in limiting access to employment. Many reported negative experiences in seeking work, and tales were often heard of discrimination, resulting in unemployment. This creates a vicious circle, discouraging some disabled people from accessing the labour market. Disabled people expected to come across negativity with employers, and so discrimination became a self-fulfilling prophecy:

> 'I'm confident that I would experience a lot of negativity
> from people that employ you, or people that are interviewing
> you.' (Focus group participant)

As a result, this man had decided not to seek paid work but worked on a voluntary basis for a disabled people's organisation, which gave him status and identity as a disabled person. While this was undoubtedly a positive choice, it was made against a background of wider labour market exclusion, discriminatory recruitment practices, a severe lack of appropriate and accessible information and being seen by employers as 'expensive' to employ. These factors all conspire to deter disabled people from entering the job market.

In a situation where special education has often under-equipped disabled adults for the contemporary job market, one disabled consultant said that he thought more needed to be done to help overcome such 'internal' barriers and get disabled people to a point where they believed that they could work:

> 'You know, if you're constantly told "don't expect to amount
> to much, don't expect to achieve too much, don't expect
> to be able to do this" – well, what are you going to think
> at the end of all that?' (Disabled consultant)

Disabled consultants felt that things were changing and that disabled children in mainstream schools might be more likely to be encouraged to work. High-profile, positive role models could help, but they felt that there were also dangers in raising expectations too high:

> 'If you get this whole message that you're just like everybody
> else actually, except that you're blind. If you work hard,
> pass exams, dress appropriately … the world will treat you

just like anybody else. And it's a lie, they don't.' (Disabled consultant)

Arthur and Zarb (1995) maintain that the process of getting a job is the most difficult stage of employment for disabled people because of direct discrimination and other barriers. Deaf and disabled people can become marginalised by the failure to meet their access needs. Already disadvantaged by their impairments, many focus group respondents felt they were doubly disadvantaged within the workplace by the lack of flexible work practices and an inability to access skills training, thus inhibiting promotion and progression prospects. They pointed out that it may be more difficult for them than their non-disabled peers to access training, as just doing their job may take their whole attention and energy, leaving no spare capacity for training as currently organised.

A key finding was that while the inflexibility of Incapacity Benefits was seen by many disabled people as a barrier to seeking employment, it was valued as a means of giving enhanced benefit rates necessary for a decent standard of life. However, these rates are threatened by the replacement of Incapacity Benefit for new claimants with the Employment Support Allowance in 2008. This inflexibility was particularly evident for some groups of people with learning disabilities (Beyer et al, 2004), particularly those who live in residential care homes, who often depend on Incapacity Benefit and a range of other benefits to fund their support needs in life. In a recent evaluation of the NDDP (Adelman et al, 2004), the main reported bridge to employment is the knowledge that disabled people can be sure of a return to benefits if their job does not work out well. A person with high costs (due, for example, to a physical impairment) should still be able to work. This means that benefits need to cover the real cost of disability, and to ensure that any employment that people seek on top of their benefits will really make an additional contribution to their income.

Although there are common themes in combating discrimination and exclusion, disability has some unique features. These include the costs of adaptations, issues in accessing information and the low expectations that come from treating people as objects of pity, or as 'ill'. The need to move from a focus on care to social participation and employment, already identified for people with learning disabilities (SCIE, 2006), has a wider relevance for disabled people generally. The key policy messages are:

- a coordinated, joined-up and person-centred approach, grounded in an individual's goals for themselves;

- the need for staff training and support on equalities issues;
- celebration of positive role models to encourage greater optimism among employers, agencies, other workers and disabled people themselves.

The emerging policy emphasis to differentiate between those who 'can' and 'can't' work through the 2007 Welfare Reform Act constitutes a crude instrument, and one that is not consistent with the progressive principles identified above. Criticisms of the NDDP initiative, a significant part of the government's welfare-to-work strategy, were borne out by our focus group's responses: low take-up, 'cherry-picking' of more able clients, little in-work support by job brokers and a lack of engagement by employers within the scheme (Stafford, 2005; Watson et al, 2005; Stafford et al, 2006). Roulstone (2000) argues that the NDDP, in failing to acknowledge the weight of employment barriers and the need to listen to disabled people's voices, has misrepresented the 'problem' of disabled people's unemployment. While the NDDP originally embodied a social model of disability, this promising start was not adequately translated into clear practices, and adds to a long list of schemes, programmes and benefits that often work against each other.

Barriers identified by reflection on wider issues of society

Through the course of this SEQUAL research project, the Deaf and disabled people who were centrally involved took part in many processes that enabled them to situate their thinking within wider societal trends. Specifically, they took part in group discussions, presentations at SEQUAL conferences, guided discussions based on the project findings, co-writing and the final dissemination conference. Through these processes, some very different ideas about the barriers to employment emerged, portraying wider views of equality. It was clear that disabled people felt that employment initiatives were tokenistic and often did not lead to 'real' and meaningful jobs. They wanted to access the same job market as everybody else and not to feel, as a member of one of the focus groups put it, "excluded from [the job market] because you are a disabled person".

Some participants reported positive experiences of employment training schemes, feeling in control of the support offered, which enabled them to work to the best of their abilities. However, many other participants had not had good experiences and were left feeling their hopes had been raised, only to then be stuck in an endless cycle of training and work experience, with no proper job at the end of it all.

Despite their many negative experiences in accessing employment, those people whom we interviewed who had worked, or were currently working, were enthusiastic about the benefits of paid employment. For example, one male focus group member said:

> 'Well it's about having a life isn't it? The motivation to do something ... sort of a social thing and self-esteem is important.... It's the thing that keeps me functioning.'

Types of provisions that had helped them to have successful working lives included personal assistance and financial support to ensure equal access to training opportunities. They insisted that these should not be special concessions for disabled employees, but rights available to everyone. As an illustration of this, one participant in a focus group spent 14 years working in a pre-Disability Discrimination Act and extremely 'disabling environment'. She worked without the support of a personal assistant (PA) and talked of having to ask colleagues for support if she needed documents brought up from the archive, or even if she wanted a hot drink. She later found a job with employers (a local disability organisation) who made it their first priority to meet her access needs and she said that this "made a huge difference to my capabilities", as an employee, rather than as a disabled person.

The Deaf and disabled consultants and focus group members were particularly critical of the dominance of individualised employment support. While there is clear evidence that employer attitudes and practices are the most significant barrier to the employment of disabled people, we found very few employment initiatives that worked with employers to change attitudes. For instance, employers may fear the image that disabled employees will bring to the workplace, and that they will not be good for business. However, positive examples of disabled employees who succeed can help to change attitudes. One project that did do this had considerable success in supporting disabled people into meaningful work. However, many employment initiatives argued that they did not have the time or resources to do so. As one of the managers put it, "no, that's not our role. I would love it to be, absolutely!".

Several projects stated they had previously worked with employers and human resources personnel, but regretted that they were no longer funded for it. Instead, employment initiatives typically worked in line with the individualised medical model. They were driven by targets of getting 'people into jobs' so assumed they should be focused on changing and developing individual employability. While many sought to do this in flexible and supportive ways, they did not see themselves as having a wider remit of trying to change the employment context.

Not all disabled people want to work full time, or in traditional workplaces, so it is positive that the emerging shift to flexible labour markets matches the wishes of some disabled people. Changes to technology, for example, which facilitate home-based work, can suit some disabled people. Some respondents, particularly people with learning disabilities, did not consider a positive working life as being just about a 9 to 5 job, but also about overcoming isolation and making social contacts, participating in and contributing to society, and exercising a degree of control (Williams et al, 2003). These effects indicate that welfare-to-work initiatives should have broader objectives than simply getting people into jobs. In the 'new' labour market, benefits systems need to respect disabled people's choices to undertake voluntary work, or part-time or full-time paid work, or a combination of these. The emphasis should be on facilitating social participation generally, including a range of paid and non-paid work options.

Our research has shown that a labour market open to all is still far from being achieved. The 1998 Human Rights Act is an advance that spurs disabled people to think in terms of rights rather than charity. However, Ellis (2005) argues that civil and human rights do not go far enough in addressing the social rights of disabled people. She argues that the shift from social rights to individualistic legal human rights is 'consistent with neo-liberal ideology underpinning welfare retrenchment across advanced industrialised countries' (Ellis, 2005, p 693). Nevertheless, social rights and human rights approaches can be mutually reinforcing, for example by extending disabled people's social rights to direct services and direct payments under their control through enforcement of Human Rights Act obligations on public authorities. The new Disability Equality Duty, which came into force in December 2006, will go some way towards further embedding equality for disabled people into the culture of organisations and workplaces. Employment and human rights issues are taken up more generally in Chapter Eleven later.

Learning from other disability policy arenas

It is clear that policies and practices in some areas have gone a long way to change attitudes, systems and values. Employment legislation needs to keep pace with other forms of policy improvements and 'modernisation'. For instance, the move towards individual budgets and direct payments means that many disabled people are now employers in their own right (PMSU, 2005). They are working with personal assistants whom they employ. Recent research reveals that this new form of employment can be rewarding, both for the employer and the employee, with personal assistants benefiting greatly from a more fulfilling form of individual support work. Moreover, the disabled person is now in a position of control and power (Leece, 2006). This can make a considerable difference to how that person is viewed within the workplace.

Further, if disability-related budgets are combined, as is recommended in the Green Paper *Independence, wellbeing and choice* (DH, 2005), Access to Work money will be seen as part of an individual's overall support cost. This means that, potentially, the same PA could support someone in their home situation and at work. In order to embrace the range of 'new' and more flexible working patterns, a new form of holistic thinking has to be adopted, where disabled people's lives are no longer compartmentalised into service-related structures, such as 'day' and 'residential' services. This may require a rethink at commissioning level, whereby commissioners start to work out the costs at the level of the individual, rather than at the level of block services. A recent review of day opportunities for people with learning disabilities (SCIE, 2006) underlined the importance of holistic, joined-up thinking at commissioning and strategic level.

At practice level, much can be learnt from the learning disability arena, where there is a switch from specialist, segregated services towards community-based opportunities and open employment (DH, 2001). 'Supported employment' has been the most effective model for getting people with learning disabilities into open employment. This approach 'adds to' and takes direct action within the existing employment market. It goes further than simply preparing the individual and then launching them at a pre-existing job market. Specifically, supported employment:

- works directly with employers to promote the commercial and other benefits of job applicants;
- supports the employee once in employment to learn and gain confidence through 'job coaches';
- phases the withdrawal of external support to allow 'natural' systems to take their place.

However, despite having demonstrated the effectiveness of this system for nearly a decade for people with learning difficulties, the government has been slow to fund it or to spread the ideas beyond the learning disability field. This is indicative of a general failure to support vulnerable people once in employment, and may also represent an ideological issue, where employment is seen as part of the package provided through social services day care (Beyer et al, 2004). A review of community-based day opportunities (SCIE, 2006) showed some examples of promising practices in shifting the balance from care towards active participation in employment. In one area of the UK, North Lanarkshire, staff who previously worked in day centres have been successfully retrained as job coaches within the supported employment model. Instead of working with clients within the day centre, their work is now individualised. Worries about benefits have not been ignored, but people are encouraged to go for 'real' jobs over 16 hours a week, and take advantage of tax credits:

> 'We've got 110 people in jobs, over 16 hours – and on the right rate of pay for the job they do. The average is 25 hours a week, and financially the average is that each individual is £101 better off each week. So many people say that people's benefits will be affected, but that's not true – you can do it.' (Supported employment manager: data from SCIE, 2006, p 7)

Finally, employment policy could learn much from other disability policy in becoming more inclusive of the views of Deaf and disabled people themselves. Our research has highlighted the value of listening closely to disabled people's views of their welfare and employment problems and needs. It was valuable to spend time with employment initiatives and to find out what they offered, but significant lessons were only learnt by listening sensitively to the views of disabled people themselves. Overall, the conclusions were that there is an excessive emphasis on supporting the disabled person to 'adapt' to the current labour market. Our respondents echoed the criticisms of contemporary disabled commentators who point to the importance of prioritising systemic change (Gibbs, 2005; Roulstone and Barnes, 2005).

A number of practical solutions emerged at the mainstreaming event held in Bristol at the conclusion of the SEQUAL research. This event had participation from disabled people, local employment initiatives, disability groups and policy makers, including a representative from the Department for Work and Pensions. The overriding conclusion was that the positive employment of disabled people requires positive changes to the workplace, including physical changes (for example, better work spaces, physical access and lifts), but attitudinal and institutional changes are also needed (for example, valuing all employees, listening and involving employees, more collaboration and teamwork). There was a clearly expressed need to focus less on the individual disabled person, and to work with employers to develop positive employment practices for disabled people and employees generally. In order for this to be effective, there was a need for strong partnerships between local employers (including the Chamber of Commerce), disabled people's organisations and job centres to be formed, in order to spread information and coordinate local change. Participants suggested that job seeking is hindered by recruitment practices and suggested, for instance, that improvements could be made to levels of information expected on CVs, and interviews could be more adapted to the needs of people with learning and other disabilities. Finally, there was a suggestion that Access to Work grants by Jobcentre Plus could be better ring-fenced by employers. The particular difficulties experienced by small- and medium-sized enterprises (SMEs) in implementing equalities training were noted, with suggestions that they could potentially pool resources. These solutions reflect the views of disabled people that systemic change is needed to overcome barriers to employment. It is hoped that their views will be matched by action.

Conclusion

This chapter has reviewed some of the current literature on the disability–employment paradox, in the light of the SEQUAL research. We have seen that disabled people are becoming increasingly empowered, within their own personal and working lives. Not only are they able to contribute their skills within the existing structure of employment, but also new forms of individualised support are giving them the opportunity to direct their own personal assistance, so that they can carry out their job more autonomously.

However, there are still considerable barriers facing Deaf and disabled people who want to work. As shown in this chapter, the many policies targeting disabled people do not appear to have had the desired effect in increasing employment levels. On the whole, this project supports the thesis of Roulstone and Barnes (2005) in underlining the importance of systemic, societal solutions to the problems of employment for disabled people. If individual disabled people are seen as 'the problem', then solutions will always be aimed at fixing that problem, and retraining people for an inflexible job market. Deaf and disabled people in the SEQUAL research want more than that. They want to be able to participate in an inclusive work environment that takes account of everyone's differing needs, to have the right not to lose out financially by choosing to work, to be able to access the same education and training as other job seekers, and also to have the right to work in a flexible job market, where part-time, home-based work and other flexible practices enable them to participate on a more equal footing. Rather than viewing social diversity as an expensive and unnecessary extra, it should be embraced positively by the labour market.

Our first recommendation therefore would be to continue to reform the benefits system, so that it provides a safeguard for the costs of living with a disability. That safeguard should be compatible with part-time, flexible or even with voluntary work, and disabled people should not be discouraged from work by the threat of losing Incapacity Benefit. Work should always pay without disadvantaging people outside the labour market, and the additional costs of living with a disability should be discounted from the equation. Second, it would be useful if employment policy and strategy could learn the lessons from direct payments. Through shifting the source of finances from social services to individual people, direct payments has changed the way in which disabled people can control their lives. If this were extended further into the workplace, disabled employees could have a stronger profile as employers in their own right. They would also be recognised as having strengths to offer, rather than just being seen as expensive liabilities. A final recommendation for policy makers and planners is to include the views and solutions that disabled people themselves advocate. That inclusion should happen through organisations run by disabled people themselves, so that they can literally become partners in formulating policy for the future. This is happening, arguably, to a greater extent in social care than in employment policy. Lessons could be learnt by more joined-up thinking, both at central government and at regional level.

The SEQUAL research has particularly underlined the importance of conducting research with disabled people and other end-users, firmly situated within the social model of disability and an understanding of societal barriers. The inclusion of individual disabled people in research can sometimes emphasise individual experience and individual solutions rather than a wider social critique. Therefore it is necessary to directly involve representatives of disabled people's organisations. Furthermore, through the actual processes of doing research, people can become more politicised and can develop their thinking about developing a more inclusive society. A new and more flexible employment scene will benefit greatly from the contributions of disabled people, and this chapter has shown how disabled people themselves can help to create that vision.

Note

[1] Members of the Sign Language community use the capital 'D' to distinguish themselves from deaf people using other forms of communication and also generally from disabled people, defining themselves as a linguistic minority.

References

Adelman, L., Kazimirski, A., Legge, K., Mangla, J., Pires, C., Reyes de Beaman, S., Shaw, A. and Stafford, B. (2004) *New Deal for Disabled People: Survey of registrants – Report of cohort 1 waves 1 and 2*, DWP Report 213, Loughborough/London: Centre for Research in Social Policy/National Centre for Social Research.

Arthur, S. and Zarb, G. (1995) *Measuring disablement in society: Barriers to employment for disabled people*, Working Paper 4, Leeds: Centre for Disability Studies, University of Leeds.

Beresford, P. (2003) *It's our lives: A short theory of knowledge, distance and experience*, London: Citizen Press.

Beyer, S., Grove, B., Schneider, J., Simons, K., Williams, V., Heyman, A., Swift, P. and Krijnen-Kemp, E. (2004) *Working lives: The role of day centres in supporting people with learning disabilities into employment*, DWP Research Report 203, London: Department for Work and Pensions.

Campbell, J. and Oliver, M. (1996) *Disability politics: Understanding our past, changing our future*, New York, NY: Routledge.

DH (Department of Health) (2001) *Valuing People: A new strategy for learning disabilities for the 21st century*, London: DH.

DH (2005) *Independence, wellbeing and choice: Our vision for the future of social care for adults in England*, Social Care Green Paper, London: The Stationery Office.

DWP (Department for Work and Pensions) (2002) *Pathways to work: Helping people into employment*, London: DWP.

Ellis, K. (2005) 'Disability rights in practice: the relationship between human rights and social rights in contemporary social care', *Disability and Society*, vol 20, no 7, pp 691-704.

Gibbs, D. (2005) 'Employment policy and practice: a perspective from the disabled people's movement', in A. Roulstone and C. Barnes (eds) *Working futures: Disabled people, employment and social inclusion*, Bristol: The Policy Press, pp 193-206.

Leece, J. (2006) '"It's not like being at work": a study to investigate stress and job satisfaction in employees of direct payments users', in J. Leece and J. Bornat (eds) *Developments in direct payments*, Bristol: The Policy Press, pp 189-204.

Oliver, M. (1990) *The politics of disablement*, London: Macmillan.

Oliver, M. (1997) 'Emancipatory research: realistic goal or impossible dream?', in C. Barnes and G. Mercer (eds) *Doing disability research*, Leeds: The Disability Press, pp 15-31.

Oliver, M. (2004) 'If I had a hammer: the social model in action', in J. Swain, S. French, C. Barnes and C. Thomas (eds) *Disabling barriers – Enabling environments*, London: Sage Publications, pp 7-12.

Piggott, L., Sapey, B. and Wilenius, F. (2005) 'Out of touch: local government and disabled people's employment needs', *Disability and Society*, vol 20, no 6, pp 599-611.

PMSU (Prime Minister's Strategy Unit) (2005) *Improving the life chances of disabled people: Final report*, London: PMSU.

Roulstone, A. (2000) 'Disability, dependency and the New Deal for Disabled People', *Disability and Society*, vol 15, no 3, pp 427-43.

Roulstone, A. and Barnes, C. (eds) (2005) *Working futures: Disabled people, employment and social inclusion*, Bristol: The Policy Press.

SCIE (Social Care Institute for Excellence) (2006) 'Having a good day? Review of community-based day opportunities for people with learning disabilities', London: SCIE (www.scie.org.uk).

Stafford, B. (2005) 'New Deal for Disabled People: what's new about New Deal?', in A. Roulstone and C. Barnes (eds) *Working futures: Disabled people, employment and social inclusion*, Bristol: The Policy Press, pp 45-58.

Stafford, B., Adelman, L., Hill, K. et al (2006) *New Deal for Disabled People: Second synthesis report – Interim findings from the evaluation*, DWP Report No 377, London: The Stationery Office.

Stanley, K. (2005) 'The missing million: the challenges of employing more disabled people', in A. Roulstone and C. Barnes (eds) *Working futures: Disabled people, employment and social inclusion*, Bristol: The Policy Press, pp 29-44.

Warren, J. (2005) 'Disabled people, the state and employment: historical lessons and welfare policy', in A. Roulstone and C. Barnes (eds) *Working futures: Disabled people, employment and social inclusion*, Bristol: The Policy Press, pp 301-14.

Watson, D., Williams, V. and Wickham, C. (2005) *A valued part of the workforce? Employment and disabled people*, Guildford: SEQUAL Development Partnership, University of Surrey.

Williams, V., Tarleton, B., Watson, D. and Johnson, R. (2003) *Nice job – if you can get it: Work and people with learning difficulties*, Bristol: Norah Fry Research Centre/Centre for Access and Communication Studies, University of Bristol.

Zarb, G. (1992) 'On the road to Damascus: first steps towards changing the social relations of research production', *Disability, Handicap and Society*, vol 7, no 2, pp 125-38.

FOUR

Between work and tradition: minority ethnic women in North West England

Stuart Speeden

This chapter takes as its central focus the relationship between minority ethnic women and employment in North West England. In terms of labour market activity, this group represents one of the least active sections of the population and therefore one of the greatest challenges to current initiatives to increase workforce participation. The analysis presented here is based on case studies constructed from interviews with project staff across a number of community projects in North West England and West Yorkshire.

The purpose of the SEQUAL research was to explore 'promising practices' that were being applied through the community and voluntary sector that could have wider application in improving labour market opportunities. The issues explored here are mostly concerned with women originating from South Asia or having a South Asian heritage and the text often refers specifically to Pakistani and Bangladeshi women. In reality, the projects deal with a much broader range of women from different origins and backgrounds but the issues encountered were similar. Pakistani and Bangladeshi women represent the largest minority ethnic groups in North West England and they also have the lowest labour market activity measured in recent surveys (Botcherby, 2006; CRE, 2006; Heath and Cheung, 2006).

The objective here has been to outline some of the 'promising practices' that have emerged from the research and locate them within a context that reflects the barriers that have to be overcome in extending labour market participation. The SEQUAL research shows the importance of community-based initiatives (CBIs) in improving 'employability' for women through a holistic framework that can help to overcome the complex social and cultural barriers that prevent access to training and the development of skills. The role played by community projects is not only to provide training and support but also a framework for negotiating between, on the one hand, values of tradition, culture and religion and, on the other, the implicit values associated with the 'citizen-worker' that is at the core of welfare and labour market reform. The research also raises problems about the notion of employability as the only factor in widening labour market participation. The qualitative accounts given by project staff and women involved in these projects point to the limitation of measures to improve employability where employment opportunities are restricted. Structural factors within the local economy, the organisation of work and the persistence of discrimination all circumscribe job opportunity. In dealing with these issues, the negotiation of citizenship and employment opportunity confronts questions both of human rights and the settlement of conflicting rights.

Minority ethnic women in the North West England labour market

North West England has a diverse minority ethnic population with widely differing backgrounds and histories of settlement. These different origins and histories contribute to widely different experience in employment and employability. In national studies, it has been widely recognised that Pakistani and Bangladeshi women have the lowest labour market activity levels in the UK (Heath and Cheung, 2006). Although the overall pattern of settlement for the Pakistani/Bangladeshi population is spread across the UK there are very significant clusters of settlement in North West England, including West Yorkshire. At a regional level, this group are by far the most numerous minority ethnic population in North West England, and this is therefore one of the largest clusters of Pakistani/Bangladeshi settlement in the UK (Table 4.1).

Among the minority ethnic population there is a relatively high proportion of people from groups that are least successful in employment terms within the UK and in particular there is a relatively high proportion of women from a Pakistani background. Recent analysis based on national statistical surveys shows that just over 25% of Pakistani women were economically active in 2001-04 compared with 70% of white women and 85% of white men (Heath and Cheung, 2006). A study undertaken in Oldham, one of the case study areas, broadly reflects this national picture (Dale et al, 2002). Unemployment among Pakistani/Bangladeshi women in the period 1993-2001 averaged 19.8% compared with 5.1% for white women and 6.9% for women from an Indian background (Heath and Cheung, 2006), and this should be seen against the background of already much

Table 4.1: Distribution of BME population in the UK, London and North West England, 2001 (%)

	UK	London	North West England
White	92.12	71.15	94.44
Mixed	1.15	3.15	0.93
Indian	1.79	6.09	1.07
Pakistani	1.27	1.99	1.74
Bangladeshi	0.48	2.15	0.39
Other Asian	0.42	1.86	0.22
Black Caribbean	0.96	4.79	0.30
Black African	0.83	5.28	0.24
Black Other	0.17	0.84	0.08
Chinese	0.42	1.12	0.40
Other	0.39	1.58	0.20
All minority ethnic groups	7.88	28.85	5.56

Source: ONS (2001)

lower than average activity rates. For those in employment, occupational attainment is lower for Pakistani/Bangladeshi women with a lower than average number in professional and managerial occupations and a corresponding higher than average number in semi-routine and routine occupations. Because of high unemployment, low pay and part-time working among Pakistani/Bangladeshi males, women are likely to be living in households that have low incomes and high dependency on benefits (Simpson et al, 2006). In all respects, therefore, Pakistani women constitute one of the major challenges for policies to widen labour market participation.

Work and traditional values

The research was concentrated in areas that had initially attracted migrants in the 1960s to work, largely, in textile industries that have subsequently experienced continuous decline. Patterns of social exclusion (SEU, 2004) prevail across the study areas with economic decline, housing and educational opportunity combining with cultural, social and religious traditions that frequently lock minority ethnic women out of the labour market.

Characteristics of exclusion may have local differences, but the complex patterns that exist within these communities need to be understood as a set of interrelated and reinforcing processes that form a barrier to work, linking culture, gender and class.

Education and educational opportunities were widely regarded within the projects as the primary route to improved employment opportunities and much of the work emphasised the development of individuals through access to qualifications. This strategy is consistent with current research on the relationship between education and employment. The link between educational attainment and success in the labour market is well documented and improvements in education are seen as a central goal within the government's Social Inclusion Strategy: 'The single most critical determinant of lifelong human capital levels is the quality of schooling a person receives. It is a hard task for post-compulsory education to compensate fully for poor attainment in school' (SEU, 2004, p 52).

Within the study areas, there was a high incidence of socio-economic deprivation and this has been linked with worklessness by the Prime Minister's Strategy Unit, who have argued that minority ethnic groups are 'disproportionately concentrated in areas of deprivation, which are often characterised by factors that correlate with worklessness' (2003, p 8). Socio-economic deprivation is seen as a contributory factor affecting success in obtaining qualifications and subsequent employment, thus increasing disadvantage (Pathak, 2000). Other contributory factors are family size and composition, as Asian families tend to be large and multi-generational (Berthoud, 1998; Connor et al, 2004) and this may result in a high proportion of minority ethnic groups having to claim Income Support, Council Tax Benefit or Housing Allowance (Berthoud, 1998). Both Pakistani and Bangladeshi households are often overcrowded and confined within older low-cost owner-occupation leading to segregation and cultural concentration (Ansari, 2002).

Settlement patterns and economic disadvantage are linked to the patterns of inward migration associated with Black and minority ethnic (BME) communities. A large part of the Pakistani community within the North West migrated to take up jobs in the textile industries of north and east Lancashire. This led to settlement in towns such as Oldham, Bolton, Rochdale, Burnley, Blackburn and Preston. The decline of the textile industries and the general rise in unemployment within these areas has led to high rates of unemployment within the minority ethnic communities (Berthoud, 1999). New patterns of economic development within the region have favoured the major cities rather than the small towns, which are locked into a pattern of economic stagnation or decline. These patterns of economic change combine with some of the social and cultural factors outlined above to produce communities that have a weak skill base for emerging industry and are locked into unemployment and low income. Strong ties to the local community and limited mobility exacerbate this situation.

Language is widely recognised as a significant barrier for access to education, training and employment for minority ethnic groups (PMSU, 2003; Connor et al, 2004; Lindley and Dale, 2004). In the SEQUAL research, project workers identified language as a continuing issue for minority ethnic women. Linguistic barriers are not only a consideration for older, first-generation migrants; they were also important for many younger women. One explanation of this was that there was a continuous inflow of young women into the study areas through marriage within the extended family, often with a wedding in Pakistan (Dale et al, 2002). And language fluency within some second- and third-generation households may be affected because English is not used in the home.

Language problems not only have an adverse impact on areas such as integration within the workforce and earning levels (Shields and Wheatley Price, 2002) but also in terms of applying for jobs, success at interviews and ability to travel to work, that is, accessing public transport information. Over three quarters of Bangladeshi women over the age of 25 do not speak fluent English, which has a considerable effect on their employability, particularly for first-generation Asian women (Ansari, 2002; PMSU, 2003).

Project workers saw family formation and cultural expectations not as a barrier but as a major factor in the low labour market activity for Pakistani and Bangladeshi women. Cultural experience varies considerably according to age and family background but traditional values were very strong and were often sustained by the strong ties through marriage and extended family to rural life in Pakistan. Those women who follow a traditional way of life get married at an early age, they tend to have children soon after marriage and adopt a traditional role as housewife. Within family life, women may often be isolated and have little contact with men or other women outside the family.

This means that there is very little opportunity to develop aspirations to work, let alone engage in training, education or employment. Traditional roles were not universal within the communities and there were women who were in work. Some of these were from less traditional families or were second- or third-generation women who had been through the education system in Britain. A further group of women often worked in local small businesses because the workplace was all-women. This meant that they were often working in low-paid, low-status work but the arrangements allowed them to work in an environment that took account of custom and tradition. The variety of experience within the community was extensive but the strong forces of culture, tradition and family life form a powerful force limiting involvement in work (Dale et al, 2002). Lindley and Dale (2004) point to several research studies that identify a strong link between traditional culture and work, citing the effects of age, partnership status and dependants on levels of economic activity (2004, p 3) alongside the less measurable effects of family and community expectations.

Second-generation migrants have educational and linguistic advantages that have allowed some progress for minority ethnic groups in professional and managerial jobs; this has done little to reduce the relative disadvantage of minority ethnic unemployment (PMSU, 2003). The report concludes that in the second generation of the 1990s there is no sign that matters have improved and White British–minority ethnic differentials have increased.

Improvement of school performance may have a long-term impact on the prospects for Pakistani and Bangladeshi women but progress cannot be taken for granted. Bhattacharyya et al's report summarises recent research and statistics on the position of different ethnic groups in education that indicates that proportionately more Black, Pakistani and Bangladeshi pupils are recorded as having special educational needs and that, on average, Black, Pakistani and Bangladeshi pupils perform less well than White pupils (Cunéo, 2001; Bhattacharyya et al, 2003). Pakistani and Bangladeshi minorities were found to have the least qualifications (Berthoud, 1999) and Bangladeshi, Black and Pakistani pupils achieve lower grades than other pupils, particularly at GCSE level.

An 'ethnic penalty' in employment

Educational achievement among some groups has to be set against a growing body of evidence that points towards an 'ethnic penalty' in employment. Statistical evidence over the past decade (Modood et al, 1997; CRE, 2006) shows a persistent pattern of ethnic disadvantage in employment across the UK. The pattern has been confirmed by recent research (Heath and Cheung, 2006; Clark and Drinkwater, 2007), which identifies personal and institutional discrimination as a significant cause. This is against a background where anti-discrimination legislation, in place since the 1960s, is failing to deliver equality of opportunity in employment.

The weak impact of equal opportunity policies is illustrated by comparing the changing performance of young people in their educational achievement with their achievements in the labour market. Despite legislation stretching back 30 years and extensive government initiatives, firm evidence continues to show that BME groups have not achieved equivalent progress in the labour market. This failure of legislation to prevent discrimination in employment has been underlined by a recent international study (Riach and Rich, 2002), which used experimental research to compare White and minority ethnic job applications. The study concluded that in Europe, Australia and North America discrimination against non-Whites and women is a persistent pattern where people are denied jobs purely because of their colour and sex.

This is not an issue confined to first-generation migrants. Despite significant improvements in language fluency and educational attainment, the second generation continues to struggle to compete on an equal footing with their White counterparts. Heath concludes, from his extensive research exploring this area (Heath and McMahon, 1999; Heath, 2001), that:

> In general, then, despite the equalisation in educational experience, the ethnic penalties among the second generation are of broadly similar magnitude to those in the first generation. (Heath and McMahon, 1999, p 32)

The picture among minority ethnic groups does vary considerably and Modood et al (1997) show divergence in the experience of different ethnic groups. In recent studies (Blackaby et al, 1999; PMSU, 2003; Connor et al, 2004) there is evidence that different minority ethnic groups face varying barriers to success in the labour market. Pakistanis and Bangladeshis experience the highest unemployment rates, in some cases nearly double that of the White population (Thomas, 1998; Blackaby et al, 1999; Metcalf and Forth, 2000; Owen et al, 2000; PMSU, 2003), while people with Indian and Chinese origin tend to experience relatively low unemployment rates (Owen et al, 2000; PMSU, 2003). These success rates provide an incomplete understanding of ethnicity and employment because they tell us little about different education and skills, the levels of social capital associated with different communities.

The overall pattern of the BME 'penalty' in employment conceals a range of disadvantage associated with different groups. The diverse pattern of disadvantage grows when we look at the 'intersectional' impact of gender, disability, age, religion and sexual orientation. Our research through SEQUAL shows that an understanding of this diversity is important in developing programmes that improve the capacity of individuals to compete in the labour market through training and skills development.

Community initiatives

The SEQUAL research focused on qualitative case studies as a basis for identifying innovative and 'promising practices'. These case studies demonstrate the importance of CBIs not simply as a source of innovation but as sites of contestation and negotiation between different sets of values. They provide distinctive frameworks through which women can, at one level, take up opportunities for training, education and work but they can also provide a safe environment for working through competing discourses of tradition, on the one hand, and the expectations of work and citizenship, on the other:

> 'Going out for some women is very difficult and they need to be part of an all women environment to get involved.' (Ananna Project worker)

These projects are not the only institutions through which such negotiations take place; schools, families and Mosques all contribute in different ways but in the communities we examined, they play an important role in the engagement of minority ethnic women.

The Sahara Project in Preston, as well as the Ananna Project in Manchester, provides examples of how community-based projects can attract women into training and employment by offering a range of activities. The Sahara Project centre provides a meeting place where mainly women can come into an informal setting where they can access advice, support and discussion. Group activities provide a route into meeting and talking with other women as well as affirming and recognising skills based on cookery or crafts. These activities create a welcoming and safe environment in which some women will progress to training in information technology (IT) or other formal qualifications. There is no presumption that all women will move into qualifications and education and there is a recognition that not all women will want to move into employment:

> 'Working with food ... things that have meaning in everyday life means that women will come in and meet and talk.

Later some will get involved and be drawn into courses.'
(Sahara Project worker)

Sahara provides an important gateway that can draw women out of isolation and make available opportunities that may enhance skills. Employment opportunities are explored, sometimes through the existing skills in cookery and food. Where tradition demands that women should have limited contact with men, Sahara (and the Ananna Project) have been able to tackle some of these problems by developing culturally acceptable employment, for example, through locally based small businesses, as well as starting to push at the barriers that constrain opportunities beyond the locality.

Many of the women who have been at home with children have not felt the need to learn English but this can reinforce their isolation and limit their access to employment, support and benefits. The opportunities provided by culturally acceptable employment can create a positive desire to learn English, and in some cases (for example, Sahara) this has led to increased demands on the part of men for English classes for their families.

The intervention of Sahara through a set of activities that are rooted in community needs leads towards an increase in skills and engagement with the labour market. It also creates conditions in which the conflicts between traditional values and work can be resolved. Sahara and projects like it provide a pathway for mediating between the government initiatives that seek to reform the welfare system and the cultural context of minority ethnic communities. Within this process there is a contestation of rights associated with women, culture, faith, the rights of access to employment and opportunities in employment.

A feature of Sahara and other projects that we examined was an understanding of what we described in the research as 'the journey to work'. This concept recognises that consideration needs to be given to the widely differing experiences within BME communities and between individuals. It also recognises that projects and programmes need to be tailored to the different needs of communities or parts of communities. A strength identified within some of the projects was the way in which they had developed a holistic approach to working with women where the emphasis was on addressing their needs rather than providing a one-dimensional service around training and employment.

For women in the projects, the route to employability and, ultimately, employment is very varied and there are particular barriers associated with culture, gender, location, language, age and disability. Each individual requires a programme that meets their particular needs in overcoming the barriers and in achieving appropriate levels of competency. Alongside the support for individuals, the project base, bringing together women with similar experiences, provides a supportive environment in which they share experience and develop confidence. It was important, however, in the case of all the women's projects, that they catered solely for women because an atmosphere could be created that helped in building support and in breaking down barriers.

At the start of the journey to employment some BME women may not see employment as a goal and may be discouraged by overt measures to 'include' them in the labour market, and there are benefits in working within a broader community development framework. A considerable barrier to the development of this more holistic approach was the overemphasis, through New Deal and other initiatives, on performance measures that deal with hard outcomes. Qualifications or successful job placement are insufficient to support the 'journey to work' for many of the women in the projects because they are dealing with a preparatory stage of development. This stage of development was often a prerequisite, particularly in the case of Pakistani/Bangladeshi women where many were expressing an initial disinterest in education or work. The combination of a social dimension alongside a programme that builds awareness and confidence is a way of providing an important bridge for access to education and employment. Measurements of progress need to reflect this and respond to the processes of negotiation and individual need. In this respect, they should reflect process as well as outcome and this requires improved systems for qualitative measurement. Performance indicators are needed that reflect the complex patterns of progress that are associated with the journey to work.

An overemphasis on access to employment or access to formal education may overlook the importance of projects that provide an important pathway towards work. In saying this, it would be wrong to assume that all women will choose to work, or progress into formal qualifications, but there are other benefits that may include improved access to public services, access to benefits and improved social cohesion.

Brokerage

Alongside building the confidence and capacity of individuals, a key role that projects can play is through improving the links between individuals seeking jobs and the employers. One project in the study, South Liverpool Personnel, has for over two decades provided a specialist agency to assist people from Liverpool's BME community in gaining employment. A key role is making contact with employers and ensuring that employment opportunities are made available within the community.

For those with higher qualifications the barriers to obtaining employment may rest more with employers than with the individuals. From the research, it is not clear whether cultural barriers do play a part in restricting employment for those with higher level qualifications, but there are barriers to access and some of the projects in the study operated graduate placement schemes to improve the link between graduates and employers (PACT, Manchester, and PATH, Yorkshire).

Equal opportunities

An important factor identified through project staff was the continuing significance of employer attitudes and the limits of equal opportunity practice. There has been some progress among large employers in the public and private sector towards the adoption of equal opportunities recruitment practices but there is little awareness among small- and medium-sized enterprises (SMEs). There should be greater consideration of the way employers relate to the needs of Pakistani/Bangladeshi women. While it is possible to improve access to training and skills through CBIs within minority ethnic communities, the challenge of employer discrimination is less tractable. We have seen through the discussion of the 'ethnic penalty' that improvements in education and training among BME groups do not automatically carry though into employment opportunity. There was a feeling among project workers that supply-side measures for improving employability needed to be matched by demand-side measures that recognised the needs of Pakistani/Bangladeshi women in employment.

Equal opportunities are often restricted to a limited range of recruitment and selection practices (Somerville and Steel, 1998) that have little value in addressing the needs of Pakistani and Bangladeshi women. Project staff saw the need for a broader vocabulary of practice that may involve schemes for positive action, changing perceptions and the use of compliance mechanisms to influence policy and practice in contracting organisations and partnerships. Breaking the cycle of low-paid employment will involve promoting work practices that can accommodate religion and tradition and both the Sahara and

Ananna Projects were providing a basis for bridging that discussion with employers.

The problem of employer discrimination has been widely explored by the Commission for Racial Equality through formal investigations and recent research shows employer discrimination to be a persistent problem. While there is a range of barriers to employment for minority ethnic groups, the fact remains that racial discrimination still plays a significant part in their exclusion from employment. In research for the Department for Education and Employment, Metcalf and Forth (2000) conclude that discrimination (direct, indirect and institutionalised) continues to reduce employment opportunities of minority ethnic groups.

The impact of discrimination is experienced both among low-skill groups and high-skill groups, including graduates. Despite government and employer drives to increase diversity in the workplace, minority ethnic graduates continue to be under-represented in graduate intakes of large firms. The barriers that were identified related to weaknesses in equal opportunity practices (Connor et al, 2004, p xix). They included:

- the policies of some large employers for targeting certain educational institutions for recruitment;
- the lack of minority ethnic role models;
- discriminatory practices in selection methods;
- issues around eligibility to work in the UK.

Project workers also referred to the changed climate following the 9/11 attacks and the 'war on terrorism'. New forms of prejudice and discrimination were thought to be emerging and a growing fear of 'Islamophobia' affected attitudes within the community towards work and training. The possibility of discrimination being constructed around religion, 'race' and gender emphasises the importance of more rigorous equal opportunity systems to support labour market participation.

Conclusion

Behind the discussion of traditional values and the 'journey to work' there are significant tensions around rights, authority and autonomy. The government's commitment to transform the benefit system through its New Deal and the strategic commitment to widen labour market participation through 'full and fulfilling employment' directs attention to minority ethnic communities where there is low labour market activity or high unemployment. The situation of Pakistani and Bangladeshi women is highlighted in recent research through the Department for Work and Pensions (2006) making them a potential target for initiatives to promote 'employability'. It is a feature of government programmes for welfare reform that they embrace a set of values and a concept of 'citizen–worker' (Lister, 2003) that can conflict with traditional values. The research here points to the value of community-based organisations, not just as a way of engaging women in training and employment but as a framework through which rights and values can be negotiated. The need for local structures that mediate change and allow for the effective implementation of human rights and equality legislation has a broader role than the negotiation of labour market participation and extends into current debates about community cohesion. The BME voluntary sector has a key role to play in the negotiation of citizenship and the projects described here provide exemplars for how this might be achieved.

While BME-led organisations were effective in responding to local needs among Pakistani and Bangladeshi women, project workers pointed to the weaknesses of the sector in terms of funding and capacity. Short-term and insecure funding represented a considerable problem but also the fact that they had to work inside government programmes that were top-down in the way that they described outcomes and set targets. A more stable financial structure and greater flexibility in performance targets would be valuable in supporting the 'journey to work'.

The support provided for individuals to develop skills and gain access to benefits and training is insufficient to ensure that Pakistani and Bangladeshi women can gain access to 'full and fulfilling' employment. The measures to support individual development need to be balanced by effective strategies to support equal opportunities. Welfare reform tends to emphasise supply factors as the primary tool for overcoming exclusion from the labour market. Skills training, access to education and individual capacity building are all important but they are likely to have a limited impact unless the policies begin to deal effectively with the exclusionary practices of *demand*; this means addressing employer discrimination, prejudice and equal opportunity alongside training and education.

Anti-discrimination measures have been established in law since the 1970s. This legal framework has been to protect individuals and communities against discriminatory practices. These laws, leaving aside their success or failure, have been concerned primarily with protection from discrimination rather than the establishment of rights.

For 30 years, the legal challenge to racial discrimination has largely depended on individual claims of discrimination. The cumulative effect of tribunals and legal action may have contributed to change but the evidence remains that employers, in general, have failed to seriously tackle problems of discrimination and put in place effective measures to assure equal opportunities. The 2000 Race Relations (Amendment) Act has recognised the need to develop and enforce practices that try to change the culture of organisations and measure outcomes for equal opportunity practice. This legislation is confined at present to public bodies, and new legislation would be required to extend these principles to the private sector.

References

Ansari, H. (2002) *Muslims in Britain*, London: Minority Rights Group International.

Berthoud, R. (1998) *The incomes of ethnic minorities*, ISER Report 98-1, Colchester: Institute for Social and Economic Research, University of Essex.

Berthoud, R. (1999) *Findings – Young Caribbean men and the labour market: A comparison with other ethnic groups*, York: Joseph Rowntree Foundation.

Bhattacharyya, G., Ison, L. and Blair, M. (2003) *Minority ethnic attainment and participation in education and training: The evidence*, London: Department for Education and Skills.

Blackaby, D., Leslie, D., Murphy, P. and O'Leary, N. (1999) 'Unemployment among Britain's ethnic minorities', *The Manchester School*, vol 67, no 1, pp 1-20.

Botcherby, S. (2006) *Moving on up – Ethnic women and work: Pakistani, Bangladeshi and Black Caribbean Women and Employment Survey: Aspirations, experiences and choices*, Manchester: Equal Opportunities Commission.

Clark, K. and Drinkwater, S. (2007) *Ethnic minorities in the labour market: Dynamics and diversity*, York: Joseph Rowntree Foundation.

Connor, H., Tyers, C., Modood, T. and Hillage, J. (2004) *Why the difference? A closer look at higher education minority ethnic students and graduates*, Research Report RR552, London: Department for Education and Skills.

CRE (Commision for Racial Equality) (2006) *Fact file 1: Employment and ethnicity*, Manchester/London: CRE.

Cunéo, P. (2001) *Ethnic minorities' economic performance*, London: Performance and Innovation Unit.

Dale, A., Shaheen, N., Kalra, V. and Fieldhouse, E. (2002) 'Routes into education and employment for young Pakistani and Bangladeshi women in the UK', *Ethnic and Racial Studies*, vol 25, no 6, pp 942-68.

DWP (Department for Work and Pensions) (2006) *Opportunity for all: Eighth annual report 2006*, London: The Stationery Office.

Heath, A. (2001) *Ethnic minorities in the labour market, Report to the PIU – Cabinet Office*, Oxford: University of Oxford.

Heath, A. and Cheung, S. Y. (2006) *Ethnic penalties in the labour market*, DWP Research Report 341, London: Department for Work and Pensions.

Heath, A. and McMahon, D. (1999) *Ethnic differences in the labour market: A comparison of the SARs and LFS*, Working Paper 71, Strathclyde: Centre for Research into Elections and Social Trends.

Lindley, J. and Dale, A. (2004) 'Ethnic differences in women's demographic and family characteristics and economic activity profiles, 1992-2002', *Labour Market Trends*, vol 12, April, pp 153-66.

Lister, R. (2003) 'Investing in the citizen-workers of the future: transformation in citizenship and the state under New Labour', *Social Policy and Administration*, vol 37, no 5, pp 427-43.

Metcalf, H. and Forth, J. (2000) *Race research for the future: Business benefits of race equality at work*, London: Department for Education and Employment.

Modood, T. et al (1997) *Ethnic minorities in Britain: Diversity and disadvantage*, London: Policy Studies Institute.

ONS (Office for National Statistics) (2001) *Census: Distribution of ethnic groups within regions* (www.statistics.gov.uk/statbase/ssdataset.asp?vlnk=6589&More=Y).

Owen, D., Green, A., Pitcher, J. and Maguire, M. (2000) *Race research for the future: Minority ethnic participation and achievements in education, training and the labour market*, London: Department for Education and Employment.

Pathak, S. (2000) *Race research for the future: Ethnicity in education, training and the labour market*, London: Department for Education and Employment.

PMSU (Prime Minister's Strategy Unit) (2003) *Ethnic minorities and the labour market*, Final Report, London: Department for Education and Skills.

Riach, P. A. and Rich, J. (2002) 'Field experiments of discrimination in the market place', *The Economic Journal*, vol 112, no 483, pp 480-518.

SEU (Social Exclusion Unit) (2004) *Breaking the cycle – Taking stock of progress and priorities for the future*, London: The Stationery Office.

Shields, M. and Wheatley Price, S. (2002) 'The English language: fluency and occupational success of ethnic minority immigrant men living in English metropolitan areas', *Journal of Population Economics*, vol 15, no 1, pp 137-60.

Simpson, L., Purdam, K., Tajar, A., Fieldhouse, E., Gavalas, V., Tranmer, M., Pritchard, J. and Dorling, D. (2006) *Ethnic minority populations and the labour market: An analysis of the 1991 and 2001 Census*, DWP Research Report No 333, London: Department for Work and Pensions.

Thomas, J.M. (1998) 'Who feels it knows it: work attitudes and excess non-white unemployment in the UK', *Ethnic and Racial Studies*, vol 21, no 1, pp 138-50.

FIVE

Discrimination and geographical exclusion: a case study of North West Wales

Brec'hed Piette and Rhian McCarthy

Introduction

The main argument in this chapter is that geography intensifies employment disadvantage, particularly for those who also experience other forms of exclusion and discrimination in the labour market related to, for instance, disability, or age. To evidence this claim, we will be drawing on SEQUAL research carried out in 2003-04 in North West Wales, a remote and largely rural area with a long history of poor employment prospects and significant poverty (Cloke et al, 1997). In many ways, the problems are similar to those of other rural areas in Britain such as South West England and Cumbria, and indeed rural areas in other parts of Europe. However, there are also specific employment issues that will also be considered here, arising from the distinct linguistic and cultural identity of North Wales.

A focus on location is important because social exclusion, marginalisation and disadvantage operate in different ways in different geographical areas (Lupton, 2003; Green and Owen, 2006) and rural areas in particular have characteristics affecting their local labour markets that are very different to those that prevail in most urban centres. Green and Owen (2006) demonstrate that geographical location often has an adverse effect on employment prospects with residents of inner cities and areas with a mining and industrial heritage faring the worst. The problems of employment and social exclusion in rural areas such as North West Wales are less visible statistically because of relatively small numbers, and physically because social deprivation occurs in pockets between more prosperous areas. They are nevertheless deserving of attention. In this chapter we will look particularly at the experiences of those living in rural areas in order to assess whether the labour market is indeed 'open to all'.

Previous researchers (Cloke and Little, 1997; Cloke et al, 1997; Beatty and Fothergill, 1999; Shucksmith, 2000, 2004) looking at experiences of employment and employability in rural areas have used a range of approaches in examining the linkages between employment and issues of social exclusion and disadvantage. These have included a structure–agency approach, more culturally based analyses and the construction of statistical indicators of multiple deprivations in rural areas. Our approach here follows mainly the first of these traditions as we sought to understand how the changing structures of rural North Wales had different implications for different social groups in producing advantage and disadvantage in the labour market. The main research method used was that of in-depth interviews with members from discriminated-against groups, those working with them on a range of community-based projects and with local employers (Piette et al, 2005). Our aim in these interviews was to explore the main barriers to employment in the area with particular reference to discriminated-against groups, and also to find out from these different stakeholders what they considered to be the most useful ways of overcoming these barriers. We looked both at individual experiences and at governmental and community-based initiatives (CBIs) aimed at enhancing employment opportunities for groups and individuals.

We also seek to argue here that the current Labour government's policy of emphasising the development of 'employability' in individuals and of mainly intervening on the supply side in the labour market (Peck and Theodore, 2000; McQuaid and Lindsay, 2005) is frequently inappropriate in a rural context where unemployment is more likely to be due to the lack of good quality jobs and to difficulty in reaching the work that does exist rather than to the employability of job-seeking individuals. Many of those who lack employment in North West Wales would very likely be employable in a different place, with a wider range of opportunities. Some, particularly those who have migrated into the area from other parts of the UK, may eschew the relatively limited opportunities that do exist and look to ways other than conventional employment to support themselves financially and also to provide the identity and self-esteem that conventionally comes with engagement in the labour market. Their notion of what constitutes 'employability' for them may turn out to be rather different from the narrow concepts of employability seen in much government rhetoric.

Finally, we will consider the human rights dimension to employment and will explore the view that people's 'rights' to suitable employment should not be at the expense of their 'right' to live in the area of their choice, whether this is where they have been brought up or have chosen to move to. Of relevance here is the very sensitive issue of the Welsh language requirement present in many sectors of the job market in North West Wales. There is arguably a conflict here that cannot be easily resolved between the 'rights' of local people to receive services through the Welsh language and the 'rights' of non-Welsh speakers to secure employment.

Characteristics of the rural

In order to develop the argument that there is something distinct about the problems of rural areas, it is useful to try and define what is meant by 'rurality' and to look at the characteristics of rural areas. This is not easy, as rurality encompasses many diverse notions, but some generally common factors (Horton, 2005) include low population density and size, distance from urban areas, certain types of economic activity, for example, farming and tourism, poor access to services and particular forms of land use.

There is increasing recognition by academics (Hoggart, 1990; Panelli, 2002), and by policy makers (WAG, 2000), that the traditional idea of the urban–rural dichotomy is outdated and that the lines between urban and rural are far more indistinct than previously thought.

Government reports and many academic studies tend to concentrate on the many economic and social problems experienced by rural communities pointing out that the disadvantage and deprivation of the countryside is often more hidden than that of towns and cities. However, the predominant cultural idea underlying 'rurality' probably owes more to the notion of the 'rural idyll', that is to say, the notion of the countryside as peaceful, not to say bucolic, where the pace of life is slow, the environment unspoilt, a place where affluent town dwellers seek to live in retirement, or, increasingly, from which to commute to employment in urban areas. Cloke et al (1997) argue that the 'rural idyll' is essentially an English concept, and that, traditionally, isolated rural communities in Wales have been seen as synonymous with poverty (Fleure, 1941) and outward migration. However, the idea of the rural idyll, despite being largely mythical, continues to motivate many people to migrate to rural Wales from English conurbations. It also to some extent affects the self-image of those who have always lived in rural areas, leading them to define themselves as fortunate in where they live despite fewer employment opportunities and poor access to services. There may also be an acceptance of low wages as somehow an inevitable concomitant of rural living. Connected with this, particularly in farming communities, is a tradition of self-reliance and independence with little expectation of a provision of services that are taken for granted in urban areas (Cloke et al, 1997). Incomers too may see lower wages as somehow a fair exchange for the perceived benefits of living in a rural area such as beautiful scenery, cleaner air and less crime.

Although these ideas may now be a little dated we did observe them in some of the people we spoke to. We also found some evidence of an anti-idyllic position, or rural 'horror', as it was expressed by Bell (1997), where rural living is seen as leading to loneliness and despair. One of our respondents said:

> 'If I hadn't had a car I would have been totally isolated – no way of getting over to B and no way of getting down the coast other than on a Tuesday and that was basically because there was a market on in Ll on a Tuesday, other than that you would have been absolutely, completely isolated; if you were a lone parent, I think you would have been in danger of having severe mental health issues definitely, no support mechanisms, no family or anything there.'

These perceptions of rurality are important in considering expectations of employment in rural areas that are often very different to those held by those living in urban areas (Newidiem, 2003). The rural environment is seen by those who live there both as an immediate, tangible and often restrictive context and as a frame of reference through which people compare their own experiences with those of people living in urban areas.

Employment issues in rural North West Wales

The particular area focused on in this chapter comprises four counties in North Wales, namely Ynys Môn (Anglesey), Gwynedd, Conwy and Denbighshire. The area is predominantly rural and includes the Snowdonia National Park. The local economy is typified by a narrow economic base with the key industries being agriculture, the agri-food sector, tourism and public sector employment. It faces a number of challenges – there is a legacy of industrial decline in the traditional activity of slate quarrying, and the agricultural sector is in crisis, exacerbated by panic some years ago over BSE (Bovine Spongiform Encephalopathy, or 'mad cow disease') and subsequently the foot-and-mouth epidemic. There are some chronic employment black spots such as Blaenau Ffestiniog, previously a major centre for the slate industry where there have been numerous attempts at economic regeneration over a period of at least 30 years, but with relatively little lasting success. The longer-term outlook is also uncertain. In Anglesey, the nuclear plant on the north coast will close in the next few years, and the loss of the other large employer on the island will follow in its wake. However, there are some positive features in the local economy; for example, tourism has been actively developed in recent years, and North West Wales is a growth centre for Welsh media and other cultural industries.

The three main employment-related problems are: unemployment, which is frequently hidden and found in pockets rather than across the region, low pay and outward migration. As in the rest of the UK, official unemployment in North Wales has declined in recent years and in 2004/05 (Kenway et al, 2006) the percentage of people of working age who were either ILO (International Labour Organization) unemployed or 'economically inactive but wanting to work' was around 5%. However, a high level of hidden unemployment remains (Beatty and Fothergill, 2004), with parts of rural North West Wales having rates of limiting long-term illness of more than 25% (Kenway et al, 2006).

As important an issue as unemployment, is the quality of jobs on offer, many of which are part time and poorly paid. Rural areas offer a far more restricted range of employment opportunities than urban areas and those jobs that are available tend to be poorly paid and unskilled. This means that those who lack geographical mobility are often working at levels far below their skills and qualifications. Agency workers we talked to who were responsible for implementing the government's policy of facilitating lone mothers into work gave many examples of well-qualified women being persuaded to take on poorly paid jobs in the tourist or retail sector as work of the kind that would have been appropriate for their level of qualification was just not available locally. It is not surprising then that some people will look for alternatives to the jobs that are available by, for instance, setting up their own businesses or working in the voluntary sector. In our study many of the non-working mainly single mothers that we interviewed had ambitions of this kind, saying, for instance, "I want to gain a qualification in a holistic area so that I can be self-employed" and, "I'd like to be teaching dance and be part of a community dance company where people meet regularly to practise dance, share skills, create dance, teach people in the community and perform".

There are signs here of people seeking participation in their communities in ways other than through paid work, and of rejecting the option of looking for the most easily available employment, perhaps pointing the way towards a different approach to social engagement, as suggested by Levitas (2001). Several of the more successful and interesting initiatives developed in recent years have been focused on business start-ups and entrepreneurship, particularly in areas related to tourism and food production.

Finally, like other rural parts of Britain, there are high rates of migration, both outward migration of young people in search of work and inward migration of older people choosing to settle in rural areas. The very significant outward migration of young people exacerbates the problems of rural depopulation and, to an extent, hides the lack of employment and training opportunities that exist locally, particularly for young people. The county of Anglesey, for instance, loses more young people in the 16-24 and 25-29 age groups than any other local authority in Wales (Newidiem, 2003), and this number has been increasing in recent years. Nearly all leave the area to gain work or further training, although problems in finding suitably priced housing are also a factor.

Of these three employment-related problems, only the first – a high rate of hidden unemployment in some pockets of the region – is appropriately tackled by provision aimed directly at improving people's employability. Solutions to the problem of underemployment and migration of young people are more likely to come from increasing the quality of work and training available in rural areas, and to giving young people entrepreneurial skills and assistance in setting up businesses. This need is recognised by many of the initiatives that have been set up by the Welsh Assembly Government, particularly in Communities First areas (WAG, 2005).

Barriers to work: transport and childcare

The two main barriers to employment that emerged from our research were problems with transport and lack of childcare. In rural areas, even when there are suitable work opportunities, accessing them usually requires transport. The problem of transport in rural areas is well documented (Monk et al, 1999; Alsop et al, 2002; Shucksmith, 2004). Getting to most places of employment or training is almost impossible from many rural villages without private vehicles. Those who have their own vehicle and the financial means to keep it on the road are able to overcome most of the problems involved in accessing employment and services. Indeed, increasing numbers of those living in North West Wales are working outside the area as far afield as Cheshire or Merseyside. However, for women who do not have access to a family vehicle, or young people who cannot afford to buy, tax and insure a car, or a disabled person who may not be able to drive, using public transport to get to work in a nearby town or village is the only option. Because the number of people using public transport has decreased enormously in recent years, its provision is woefully inadequate, for instance one of our respondents said:

> 'With work and training and so on, it comes down to one thing – transport and how many buses and what time those run. Very few come to B – you're better off living in M than B, everything goes through M. So if you miss the bus from D, well that's it – there's isn't another until tomorrow, and you've had it if you can't afford to pay for a taxi.'

Young people are particularly affected as many of them are likely to depend on public transport, for instance to attend college or other training centres. Lack of transport frequently restricts young people's choices of both training and work, and employers are often wary of taking on young people with long or complex journeys on public transport even when young people are themselves willing to undertake these (Furlong and Cartmel, 2000). Social class and gender issues are relevant here as not all young people are similarly affected; those from middle-class families are likely to learn to drive and to have access to a family car from a fairly young age. Driving licences are typically obtained two years earlier by middle-class young people than by working-class young people, and two years earlier by boys than by girls (Shucksmith, 2004).

Disabled people represent another group that is frequently dependent on public transport. They are more likely to find work with large employers, but these may be at some distance away from where people live. Other disabled people could find work on industrial estates, generally outside town centres, which are either inaccessible by public transport or involve complex journeys that are impossible for some disabled people. Specialist training opportunities and guidance services for disabled people are only available in a few areas.

Of course it is not only those in rural areas that face transport problems, and cost is as significant as accessibility. One of the findings of a study from Green and Owen (2006) was that those with low-level skills typically travel shorter distances to work than those with higher-level skills, both because of the practical difficulties involved and because the trade-off between wages and travel costs does not make it worthwhile. Our research was in line with this, suggesting that transport was not a problem for middle-class people even in very remote areas as road links have generally been improved and people will commute long distances particularly to desirable jobs. The problem of transport is as linked to social class as it is to geography.

In our study, the problem of affordable and accessible childcare was cited second only to transport difficulties. In fact, these two problems frequently occurred together as lone parents are a group with low levels of car ownership. Although figures seem to demonstrate (Kenway et al, 2006) that the number of childcare places per child is reasonably high in some rural counties of Wales, this does not mean that there are enough childcare places near to where people live, and at a reasonable cost. There are pockets of provision in the towns and more affluent villages where there are well-paid professionals to use them, but other areas have virtually no provision at all. In some cases, childcare provision had been set up through the efforts of volunteers in accessing project funding but this often only provided a short-term solution, as in the following example that we were given:

> 'There are more and more agencies offering more and more services in towns and there is more money available for childcare, but the reality is that the after-school club has closed because there is no funding for it – there's plenty available for setting up and nothing to run it afterwards.'

This is an important point indicating that what may be a viable solution for an urban or a relatively affluent area (money for start-up costs, but self-financing after this) is not likely to be realistic in a poor rural area. With the end of project funding for childcare, parents have to give up jobs and leave training courses. This is one of the problems that has been identified by the Welsh Assembly Government and provision is in place for training childminders in areas of identified shortages, such as Anglesey.

We were also told that many parents preferred informal childcare arrangements provided by relatives, as this was seen as more trustworthy. Similar findings have been found in other studies (Bell et al, 2005). One reason for this preference in North West Wales may be linguistic; there are very few Welsh-speaking childminders and many parents whose small children are being brought up in Welsh-speaking households will not wish to use a childminder who cannot speak Welsh.

Solutions to individuals' problems with transport and childcare are often handled by agencies on a case-by-case basis, with individual packages being designed incorporating driving lessons, vehicles purchased where required, assistance with childcare and so on. A substantial increase in funding through various employment-based initiatives that have been introduced in the past seven or eight years have made it possible for some individuals to access work outside their local area that would not have been possible previously. However, those who have to deal with multiple barriers involving lack of transport, caring responsibilities and perhaps other difficulties still find it difficult to obtain good-quality employment.

Incomers and issues of language and culture

Despite considerable outward migration, the overall population figures for the area are relatively static as the outward migration of mainly young people is matched by inward migration of older age groups. Although some of those are the relatively affluent retired, others will be younger and looking for work. The problems that the incomers face are in part those also experienced by the local population such as poor transport and lack of childcare. Inward migration also tends to occur in pockets rather than uniformly throughout the region, with some villages or parts of towns attracting significant numbers that the local limited job market cannot easily absorb. This means that people who were able to find employment in their previous areas of residence, generally in urban areas, often fail to find similar work in the new area. This is just as likely to affect professional people such as teachers as it is other non-professional and unskilled groups. As well as having problems themselves in finding suitable work, in-migration can also cause social problems (Jones, 2002). The more affluent compete with local people for limited resources such as housing, frequently pricing the locals out of the housing market in many localities. Other less socially privileged groups may be perceived as importing crime or other socially undesirable behaviour to previously harmonious rural communities. But there are positive aspects to in-migration. For instance, incomers can revitalise dying communities – several small village schools have been kept open because of the influx of children from families moving into the area and other incomers may also set up businesses that offer employment to local people. Since 2006, migrants from Eastern Europe have also arrived in fairly significant numbers, finding seasonal work in the agricultural and tourist sectors.

One of the most notable features of North West Wales is that it is a bilingual community. The numbers of Welsh speakers vary considerably across different parts of the region but in Gwynedd and Anglesey between 60% and 70% of the population were bilingual at the 2001

Census. The inward migration of non–Welsh speakers over the past four decades has led to much concern that in many localities there has been a decrease in the use of the Welsh language and a dilution in Welsh culture more generally (Cloke et al, 1997). One attempt to counter this has been through a huge increase in the teaching of Welsh in schools and a growth in the use of Welsh in a wide range of public domains. Additionally, in the past 20 years and uniquely in the context of the UK, linguistic skills in a language other than English have now become a prerequisite for many of the better paid and more desirable jobs, particularly in the public sector. This creates particular challenges for migrants to the area in that they may find that they do not meet the essential criteria for posts for which they would be well qualified in other parts of the UK, or indeed other parts of Wales, and in the context that they now find themselves lacking certain skills needed for employability. If they are already in a post, they may be required to learn Welsh; if not, they may be unable to get a post appropriate to their qualifications and experience without learning the language. There are now many adults learning Welsh whose main motivation for doing so is to improve their prospects for employment. Public sector employers will often provide classes in the workplace and release staff during working time to attend them, and employment agencies will also sponsor unemployed people to attend Welsh classes in order to enhance their chances of employment. The enthusiasm shown by some who move into the area for the local language and culture and the efforts they make to learn Welsh also add to the dynamism of these, and can make local people feel pride in an inheritance that might otherwise tend to be taken for granted.

This example of unemployed migrants who in this context are generally White English speakers makes the point quite tellingly that 'employability' is clearly linked to location. This of course mirrors the experience of refugees and migrants to other parts of Britain who are perceived to lack 'employability' in their current context despite being highly qualified for work and experienced in another part of the world.

A human rights perspective

One of the rights outlined in the United Nations Universal Declaration of Human Rights (Addis and Morrow, 2005) is the right to work. In practice, as this chapter seeks to demonstrate, this is heavily affected by where you live. In fact most people in rural areas probably do not see their right to work in the place of their choice as a human rights issue, but arguably it should be. Certainly, many of the people we spoke to expressed a sense of anger at the ways in which they felt that their rights to social inclusion and participation in the mainstream of society were not treated as seriously by policy makers in Wales as were those of people in more urban areas in the south, nearer to the Welsh Assembly Government in Cardiff and more likely to be in the constituencies of Assembly Ministers. Our respondents felt, with justification, that young people should not be obliged to leave family and friends and 'get on their bikes' to live elsewhere in order to get the kind of training and career opportunities that would be taken for granted in more populated areas elsewhere. Perhaps more controversially, it can also be argued that those who choose to move into areas such as North Wales should also have the same rights of employment, but an insistence on this right of employment by non-Welsh speakers then conflicts with the rights of Welsh speakers to obtain services through the medium of Welsh. There is no easy answer here to the conflicting rights of different groups. In other parts of the UK migrant workers generally accept that their right to work is conditional on them acquiring a reasonable skill in English to allow them to work effectively through that language. Increasingly the right to work in many occupations in North West Wales is also modified by this linguistic requirement.

Another human rights issue that particularly affects those living in geographically isolated areas is the rights of those not able to drive. This may be through choice but is more likely to be linked to some form of disability or to lack of money for driving lessons and a car. Employers in rural areas advertise many jobs as 'own transport essential' although driving is not part of the job itself. The human rights perspective of this assumption is demonstrated by a case successfully brought under UK disabilities legislation, where a person was refused employment because he did not have a driving licence even though he could have travelled by other means for the job (European Commission, 2005).

Conclusion

In focusing on North West Wales as a case study of one of the most rural areas in the UK, we have tried to demonstrate that geography has an effect on employment opportunities. However, this does not affect all equally. The resources available to middle-class rural dwellers means they are largely immune from the problems related to geographical location. However, this is not the case for the young, some women, particularly single parents, disabled people, and, above all, those who are poor. Unlike most urban areas, the poor and the affluent live in close proximity in rural areas hence the different perceptions of rural living as 'idyllic' or 'horrific'. It is not rurality per se that is the problem, but poverty. In recent years, particularly since the advent of Welsh devolution in 1997, considerable resources have been put into alleviating unemployment, by, for example, helping people to access jobs through providing training, driving lessons, cars and so on. People are also supported to set up businesses, and there have been notable successes here. However, there are still not enough good-quality, well-paid jobs. The Welsh Assembly Government has shown concern and responsiveness to some of the issues of rural social exclusion and is also prioritising public policy to tackle long-standing social divisions, discriminations and inequality. But despite itself providing many examples of promising practice it is also still working within the neoliberal constraints set by the Westminster government and its own relatively limited powers. This has perhaps prevented a sufficient emphasis on a wider view of social participation, which would not only tackle barriers to work and develop employment skills, but also provide opportunities for voluntary work, for self-employment and perhaps, ultimately, following Levitas's (2001) suggestion, remove paid employment as the central plank of their policy, issues that the book returns to later as a general issue in Chapter Eleven.

References

Addis, M. and Morrow, P. (2005) *Your rights: The Liberty guide to human rights*, London: Pluto Press.

Alsop, R., Clisby, S., Craig, G. and Hockey, J. (2002) *Beyond the bus shelter: Young women's choices and challenges in rural areas*, Oxford: Young Women's Christian Association.

Beatty, C. and Fothergill, S. (1999) *Labour market detachment in rural England*, Rural Research Reports 40, London and Salisbury: Rural Development Commission.

Beatty, C. and Fothergill, S. (2004) *Not gone, but forgotten: Real unemployment in rural North West Wales*, Bangor: Datris Marketing Research.

Bell, A., Finch, N., La Valle, I., Sainsbury, R. and Skinner, C. (2005) *A question of balance: Lone parents, childcare and work*, York: Joseph Rowntree Foundation.

Bell, D. (1997) 'Anti-idyll: rural horror', in P. Cloke and J. Little (eds) *Contested countryside cultures: Otherness, marginalisation and rurality*, London: Routledge, pp 94-108.

Cloke, P., Goodwin, M. and Milbourne, P. (1997) *Rural Wales, community and marginalisation*, Cardiff: University of Wales Press.

Cloke, P. and Little, J. (1997) *Contested countryside cultures: Otherness, marginalisation and rurality*, London: Routledge.

European Commission (2005) *Equal rights in practice*, Luxembourg: Office of European Communities.

Fleure, H. (1941) 'Foreword', in E. Bowen (ed) *Wales: A study in geography and history*, Cardiff: University of Wales Press Board.

Furlong, A. and Cartmel, F. (2000) *Youth unemployment in rural areas*, York: Joseph Rowntree Foundation.

Green, A. and Owen, D. (2006) *The geography of poor skills and access to work*, York: Joseph Rowntree Foundation.

Hoggart, K. (1990) 'Let's do away with the rural', *Journal of Rural Studies*, vol 6, no 3, pp 245-52.

Horton, M. (2005) 'Rural crisis, good practice and community development responses', *Community Development Journal*, vol 40, no 4, pp 425-32.

Jones, J. (2002) 'The cultural symbolisation of disordered and deviant behaviour: young people's experiences in a Welsh rural market town', *Journal of Rural Studies*, vol 18, no 2, pp 213-17.

Kenway, P., Parsons, N., Carr, J. and Palmer, G. (2006) *Monitoring poverty and social exclusion in Wales 2005*, York: Joseph Rowntree Foundation.

Levitas, R. (2001) 'Against work: a utopian incursion into social policy', *Critical Social Policy*, vol 21, no 4, pp 449-65.

Lupton, R. (2003) *Poverty Street: The dynamics of neighbourhood decline and renewal*, Bristol: The Policy Press.

McQuaid, R. and Lindsay, C. (2005) 'The concept of employability', *Urban Studies*, vol 42, no 2, pp 197-219.

Monk, S., Dunn, J., Fitzgerald, M. and Hodge, I. (1999) *Finding work in rural areas: Barriers and bridges*, York: Joseph Rowntree Foundation.

Newidiem (2003) *Age-balanced communities in rural Wales: Final report to the National Assembly for Wales*, Cardiff: Welsh Assembly Government.

Panelli, R. (2002) 'Young rural lives: strategies beyond diversity', *Journal of Rural Studies*, vol 18, no 2, pp 113-22.

Piette, B., McCarthy, R. and Evans, L. (2005) *A different place, a different language: The impact of geography and language in North West Wales*, Guildford: SEQUAL Development Partnership, University of Surrey.

Peck, J. and Theodore, N. (2000) 'Beyond "employability"', *Cambridge Journal of Economics*, vol 24, no 6, pp 729-49.

Shucksmith, M. (2000) *Exclusive countryside? Social inclusion and regeneration in rural areas*, York: Joseph Rowntree Foundation.

Shucksmith, M. (2004) *Social exclusion in rural areas: A review of recent research*, London: Department for Environment, Food and Rural Affairs.

WAG (Welsh Assembly Government) (2000) *The rural development plan for Wales*, Cardiff: WAG.

WAG (2005) *Wales: A vibrant economy*, Cardiff: WAG.

SIX

Out of the picture? Sexual orientation and labour market discrimination

Anne Bellis with Teresa Cairns and Susan McGrath

Introduction: the need for national and local visibility

Labour market discrimination linked to sexual orientation has received little attention by researchers and not much is known about the labour market experiences of lesbian, gay, bisexual and transgender (LGBT) people. There is no question about sexual orientation in the national Census and the collection of such information would anyway be problematic because of fears about the consequences of self-identification (Stonewall Cymru, 2004). Gay rights campaigning groups claim this lack of a research base has contributed to the marginalisation of sexual orientation within the equalities policy framework that from the 1970s onwards has focused on issues of gender, 'race' and disability. Despite the widespread discrimination experienced by LGBT people in many different aspects of their lives, legislation relating to sexual orientation was only introduced in December 2003, reflecting its low priority within the equalities 'hierarchy' (Stonewall, 2004).

This chapter focuses on sexual orientation and the labour market and its relative invisibility within discourses of discrimination and equal rights. It argues that homophobia has contributed to the general under-resourcing of research into issues of sexuality, keeping LGBT people effectively 'out of the picture' (Stonewall Cymru, 2004). The issue of labour market discrimination is located within the long-standing struggle for social, cultural and political rights by lesbian and gay community activists. Research by the SEQUAL project illuminated how such struggles for recognition are mobilised at the local grass-roots level. It explored issues of sexual orientation and discrimination in employment through a case study of the labour market experiences of LGBT people in two coastal towns in the south of England: Hastings and Brighton & Hove (Bellis et al, 2005).

The research illuminated the complex discriminatory processes that affect LGBT communities and highlighted the active role played by community organisations in tackling social exclusion, including barriers to training and employment.

The chapter argues that sexual orientation issues need to be more prominent within policies to promote labour market equality. A holistic and inclusive approach to human rights, transcending the limits of traditional equalities frameworks, could help to overcome the marginalisation of sexual orientation issues within equalities discourses.

The LGBT community and the struggle for equal rights

The emergence of the LGBT community sector in the 1980s and 1990s in the UK is the latest development in a long history of struggle and campaigning for equal rights, reaching back to the 19th century. This has taken place against the background of the social construction of 'homosexuality' as a deviation from the modern capitalist family and the narrow gender roles ascribed to men and women. Harsh legal and moral sanctions against gay sex remained in place until 1967, when the Sexual Offences Act brought about a limited degree of decriminalisation (Weeks, 1990). The subsequent growth of gay liberation in the 1970s, influenced by feminism and the Black civil rights movement, gave new impetus to the struggle for gay equal rights and helped to establish a degree of recognition for lesbian and gay people as 'an oppressed minority within capitalist society' (Weeks, 1990, p 230).

In the late 1980s, at a time when gender and 'race' equalities legislation had become established, the cause of gay equal rights was again threatened by Section 28 of the 1986 Local Government Act, which prohibited local authorities from 'promoting homosexuality' and state schools from teaching 'the acceptability of homosexuality as a pretended family relationship'. However, rather than undermining the morale of the newly emerging LGBT community, Section 28 led to a revival of lesbian and gay activism (Weeks, 1990; Palmer, 1995). Its activities rapidly diversified, including an expanding gay publishing sector, and the appearance of lesbian and gay groups within political parties and trade unions (Palmer, 1995). New campaigning organisations were formed, including Stonewall, which from the 1990s onwards has actively highlighted all forms of discrimination faced by LGBT people.

One previously neglected area that became the focus of attention in the 1990s was the discrimination and prejudice experienced by LGBT people in employment. In 1993, Stonewall's landmark survey showed that discrimination and harassment were widespread, and that many lesbians and gay men chose to conceal their sexuality in the workplace (Palmer, 1993). However, it was not until December 2003 that the first measures to combat discrimination on grounds of sexual orientation were finally introduced through the Employment Equality (Sexual Orientation) Regulations. Following the EU's 1997 Treaty of Amsterdam, the UK government was compelled for the first time to provide legislative protection to LGBT people against direct or indirect discrimination, including harassment or victimisation in the workplace. In addition, the 2004 Civil Partnership Act has addressed some of the inequalities facing same-sex couples in relation to workplace benefits, providing a range of other partnership rights previously only available to heterosexual married couples. The 2004 Gender Recognition Act recognised the legal rights of transsexual people to their acquired gender. These legislative developments represent significant shifts in public policy towards sexual orientation and gender identity issues at UK and European levels, including a growing recognition of differences within the LGBT population.

Legislation can, however, only be part of the solution to overcoming 'centuries of institutionalised homophobia' (LAGER, 2002, p 13). Recent surveys carried out by LGBT community organisations in various parts of the UK have highlighted the fact that fear of prejudice and discriminatory attitudes remain a major problem for many LGBT people in the workplace, leading frequently to concealment (Webb and Wright, 2001; Morgan and Bell, 2003; Fairley and Nouidjem, 2004). This contributes to the perpetuation of a workplace and labour market culture in which sexual orientation issues still remain largely invisible. Research has also highlighted issues of diversity and inequality within this 'community of interest' and while the term 'LGBT community' is a useful political construct, these differences should not be overlooked. A survey of LGBT people in Scotland revealed that many respondents had experienced discrimination from within the community itself because of their age, gender identity, ethnic identity or disability. As one observed:

> I don't believe there is *one* LGBT community *but many.* LGBT people are in themselves not like-minded – they are probably as good, bad, interesting, boring etc as any

other cross-section of society. (Morgan and Bell, 2003, p 15; original emphasis)

Profiling the case study localities

The University of Sussex SEQUAL research provides further evidence of the diversity identified above, and of the inequality and complex barriers experienced by LGBT people seeking to enter and progress in the labour market. It was a participatory action research project working collaboratively with local LGBT activists. This led the research team to become involved in community-based initiatives (CBIs), including participation in the UK's first LGBT Job Fair in 2004 organised by the Brighton-based partnership A Place at the Table, and in the development of a sexual orientation equalities toolkit for employers. The local research findings were later shared with LGBT organisations in other parts of the UK to test their wider relevance.

The research explored the similar and contrasting experiences of members of LGBT communities in two coastal towns – Brighton & Hove and Hastings. Despite their location in one of the most prosperous regions of the UK, both resorts have significant levels of poverty and social exclusion, including some wards among the 157 most deprived in England (Indices of Multiple Deprivation, 2004). Hastings has particularly high levels of deprivation with many characteristics typical of depressed coastal economies: a poor transport infrastructure, an ageing population and high concentrations of low pay, low skills, unemployment and 'worklessness' (New Economics Foundation, 2005). In 2004, Hastings was ranked as the most socially deprived borough in the south-east region and the 27th most deprived area in England. There are an unusually high number of small businesses, and a predominance of seasonal and casual work contributes to unemployment and economic inactivity rates significantly higher than the surrounding region.

In 2004, Hastings' LGBT population was estimated at between 3,000 and 4,700%, or 3.5%–5.5% (Fairley and Nouidjem, 2004). This fairly small and not particularly visible community appears to be typical of many other urban areas. This study found that, in common with most of the Hastings population, lifestyle choices for LGBT people were constrained by poverty and social isolation. Over a third of respondents had actively considered moving away from Hastings, with the lack of appropriate social venues in which to meet other LGBT people cited as the main reason. This was supported by comments from a gay activist in the SEQUAL research who reported that, in his experience,

LGBT people who were able to move out of Hastings were doing so "to look for higher wages and better living conditions". He added that, for those remaining in the area, travelling to gay-friendly social venues in Brighton or London was made difficult by low incomes: "Dinkies ['double income no kids'] fuel Brighton – here it's low incomes even for gay couples" (male gay activist, Hastings).

Members of an LGBT social support group based in Hastings identified some concerns of older members of the community, including pension and 'next of kin' rights, and being allowed to live together in residential care. They complained generally of an absence of services for LGBT people in the Hastings area and a lack of awareness of sexuality issues among mainstream service providers.

By contrast, Brighton & Hove in 2004 had a buoyant local economy and a much larger LGBT population. Unlike Hastings, it has successfully remained a thriving seaside resort and conference venue. While hospitality and tourism make a major contribution to the local economy, knowledge-based, creative and new media industries also account for nearly 20% of local businesses (Brighton & Hove City Council Economic Development Team, 2004). The city has a highly educated and youthful workforce, linked to the presence of around 30,000 higher education students attending local universities, with significant numbers staying on after graduation.

Estimates of Brighton's LGBT population range from 20,000 to 35,000, or 8% to 14% (Webb and Wright, 2001). This larger than average LGBT community has its roots in Brighton's reputation since the 1930s as a 'tolerant haven' for lesbians and gay men (Brighton Ourstory Project, 2001). Since the 1990s, the community's growing confidence has been associated with the development of a significant gay business sector, mainly in retail, leisure and catering, which is a prominent feature of the city's 'strong entrepreneurial culture' (Brighton & Hove City Council Economic Development Team, 2004). Local businesses target the 'pink pound', that is, the spending power of higher earning members of the LGBT community. The Brighton Gay Pride Festival is now a major annual event on the Brighton calendar, attracting thousands to the city. As a result of all this, LGBT identity is a strong element in the local authority's marketing of the city (Brighton Ourstory Project, 2001).

Nevertheless, the SEQUAL research indicated perceptions that sexual orientation issues were still marginalised in strategic policies. Interviews with workers in local equalities and community regeneration initiatives claimed that traditional approaches to equalities still predominated. One example cited was the local authority's 'inclusive city' policy:

> 'Lesbians and gay men aren't actually included in this policy because at the beginning it said its baseline data would be the Census figures of 2002, but of course we're not included in the Census ... so we're invisible.' (Male equalities worker, Brighton)

Another respondent working within a local community regeneration project felt that the lack of interest in sexual orientation shown by the regional funding body reflected a rigid focus on national concerns, and a lack of sensitivity to significant local issues:

> 'Race and ethnicity are the real focus it seems to me ... so the only questions I am asked by them are to do with race ... and within an area that has a minority ethnic population of maybe 4% ... and the number of people who are LGBT even in this area is probably about 10%.' (Female community worker, Brighton)

Sexual orientation, deprivation and social exclusion

While the deprivation in Hastings is only too apparent, the image of Brighton & Hove as a well-educated and prosperous city masks a more complex reality, associated with an emerging 'dual economy' divided between highly paid 'knowledge' workers on the one hand, and low paid workers and the long-term unemployed on the other (Brighton & Hove Economic Development Team, 2004). There is firm evidence of significant levels of poverty, social exclusion and long-term unemployment among sections of the population (Indices of Multiple Deprivation, 2004). These social problems are exacerbated by a lack of affordable housing, which 'has become a major issue for the city, affecting recruitment and retention for local employers and widening the divide between the city's rich and poor residents' (Brighton & Hove Economic Development Team, 2004). This has been linked to high levels of homelessness and rough sleepers, which are reportedly the highest outside London.

Interviews with gay activists and project workers in Brighton & Hove indicated that these social divisions were reflected in the LGBT population. Concerns were expressed that, in its enthusiasm for promoting the city as a 'gay Mecca', the council was in danger of sidelining the needs of more socially excluded LGBT people. While there was a significant migration of LGBT people to Brighton & Hove because of its reputation as a 'gay friendly' town, many experienced difficulty finding somewhere affordable to live, regular employment and sometimes were also coping with a range of health-related issues, including mental health problems, drug dependency and HIV/AIDS.

A survey of the views and needs of LGBT people in Brighton & Hove, carried out as part of consultations for the development of a local community regeneration strategy, confirmed that the LGBT community had diverse experiences, needs and aspirations. Over 21% of the sample were economically inactive – nearly a third of this group were disabled and nearly a quarter were retired (Webb and Wright, 2001). Although over half the respondents had moved to Brighton because of the existence of the LGBT community, about 20% did not have anywhere to live when they moved into the area. There was further evidence from the SEQUAL research that a significant number of rough sleepers on the streets of Brighton & Hove identified as LGBT and their sexual orientation was the principal reason for coming to the area.

The SEQUAL research findings, in both Brighton & Hove and Hastings, highlighted in particular the needs of vulnerable young people who had either identified as lesbian or gay, or were exploring their sexual identity. An interview with a sexual health outreach worker highlighted the combined effects of poverty, mental and sexual health for those who needed support in defining their sexual orientation. The respondent raised particular concerns about the 'unsafe' sexual practices of some young gay men in the area and the prevalence of casual sexual encounters with bisexual older men. He saw a need for specific outreach work with young LGBT people, describing the situation in Hastings in particular as "very closeted. It's a cultural, class issue within the deprived communities". He pointed out that in the past there had been difficulty working with young people in schools around such issues, as a result of the Section 28 legislation. Although repealed in 2003, there was still a lack of strategies for addressing issues of sexual identity in a positive and supportive way.

Respondents involved in community safety and health promotion in Brighton indicated some of the less positive consequences of the presence of a large and diverse LGBT population in the city. Community workers confirmed that many young gay men who previously may have migrated to the gay scene in London were now arriving in Brighton. Some of these had joined the city's growing number of rough sleepers and there was evidence of unsafe sexual practices among them. A project funded through the local primary healthcare trust recognised that low self-esteem was one of the contributory factors to unsafe sexual behaviour among men and was seeking to provide opportunities for gay men in Brighton & Hove to discuss these issues. A victim liaison officer in a deprived area of the city identified the particular problems faced by young gay men living on socially disadvantaged, marginal housing estates and their vulnerability to homophobic crime. He commented that moving away from their community could be equally problematic, as "if they move into hostels they can encounter the same prejudices there". He called for the provision of safe housing similar to women's refuges, for young people who needed access to services and health and welfare advice.

A significant finding from the SEQUAL research was that LGBT community organisations in Brighton and Hastings actively addressed diverse forms of social exclusion among their client groups, including barriers to training and employment. These grass-roots initiatives typically offered a holistic package of support addressing a range of needs including sexual health, mental health, community safety, victim support and social isolation. Although unemployment and labour market issues were not necessarily addressed directly or viewed as a priority (compared to more basic 'survival' needs), some voluntary organisations were delivering services designed to improve employability, while at the same time offering a 'safe space' to LGBT clients, which did not appear to be available locally through mainstream service providers. In Hastings, for example, a sexual health organisation was working in partnership with a local social support organisation for young LGBT people. The aim of the project was to offer support, including health advice, to clients who were exploring their sexual identity or those who might be suffering from homophobic bullying. Supporting what the outreach worker described as a "mobile clientele", there were contact points around the town, including a community learning centre, which offered training opportunities. The use of an open access venue such as this was viewed as a positive development, offering a much-needed 'safe space' for vulnerable young LGBT people.

In Brighton, two LGBT support groups had worked in partnership to devise and deliver a programme of vocational training to people diagnosed as HIV positive. While a positive diagnosis does not indicate sexual orientation, there was evidence that the majority of HIV positive people in Brighton & Hove were gay White men. Access to appropriate employment advice and training is an important issue for people with HIV status. For example, they may not be ready to return to full-time work and require more flexible work situations, raising issues about eligibility for sickness benefits. Others may decide to seek retraining, skills updating or a change of employment. The training programme offered a package of vocational training, careers advice, guidance and job search skills tailored to meet the particular needs of HIV members of the LGBT community. One of the partner organisations also offered training in arts and new media technologies to LGBT people in Brighton, skills particularly relevant to the local labour market. Through their involvement in a local advice and information network, they also delivered equalities training to other advice and guidance workers about working with LGBT people, thus mainstreaming their considerable experience.

Despite the important role played by LGBT organisations in addressing issues of employability linked to sexual orientation, many of them faced major challenges in terms of limited and short-term funding, and a lack of capacity and infrastructure. Some of the community workers we interviewed expressed concern that the fragmented nature of project funding had made long-term planning of work to support LGBT client groups difficult to sustain. This point was reinforced by the closure of the arts and media training organisation described above, shortly after the completion of the SEQUAL research.

By contrast, the research found evidence that mainstream training programmes were not generally regarded as offering a 'gay friendly' environment. According to staff from training organisations working with socially excluded groups, the use of homophobic language and behaviour by many trainees was commonplace, for example as in the use of the terms 'gay' or 'queer' as casual insults. One respondent commented that the preponderance of White working-class men on such training programmes could make the environment insufficiently safe for LGBT trainees to be open about their sexuality.

The SEQUAL research reinforced the criticisms that have been made of approaches based on narrow 'supply-side' concepts of employability and 'job readiness', which fail to take into account the complex social factors that disadvantage particular groups of people in the labour market (McQuaid et al, 2005). The findings of these local case studies suggest that a broader approach to developing employability skills would be more appropriate for some vulnerable groups of LGBT people seeking employment. This would recognise the need for creating more favourable labour market conditions for disadvantaged groups, such as the provision of training environments for young people where issues of sexuality and sexual health could be safely explored, and where homophobic attitudes and negative stereotypes of LGBT people could be challenged.

Widespread homophobia in the workplace

Many examples from the SEQUAL research illustrate the insidious ways in which homophobia and fear of homophobia can negatively impact on equality in the workplace, leading to self-censorship and concealment among LGBT employees. For example, a public sector union representative, also a gay activist, pointed out that the difficulties faced by lesbian or gay frontline workers can be exacerbated by lack of support from colleagues and managers:

> 'We have a member who works in a family centre ... she's an out lesbian and everyone thinks that's great ... her colleagues do ... but she's not out to her client group ... because she doesn't feel safe ... she doesn't feel there's support from colleagues because ... when you talk about issues of safety and oppression ... then people don't want to know ... it's not seen as an issue for the employer – it's an issue for the individual lesbian or gay man who is providing a frontline service.' (Male union representative, Brighton)

The class and gender dimensions of safety in the workplace were also identified by an equalities worker who discussed the difficulties of 'coming out' in local authority occupations dominated by traditional male working-class cultures (for example, electrical and maintenance, refuse collection) as opposed to more typically middle-class areas of work:

> 'There are pockets in the authority where it is not safe to be out, and those are traditional areas around building control, surveyors ... we have one member who's had a lot of homophobia, who works in the electrical and maintenance section ... the same with the big refuse section, these are all traditional, male working-class areas, but if you work in social services or ... policy or strategy areas, a bit more off the front line, it's a lot more acceptable ... a lot safer.' (Male equalities worker, Brighton)

Another employment field in which it was problematic for lesbians and gay men to feel open about their sexual identity was working with children or young people as teachers or play workers. One community worker in Hastings commented on terms such as 'gay' and 'paedophile' being commonly directed towards male childcare workers and the negative impact such stereotyped views were likely to have on young men, gay or heterosexual, thus reinforcing gender segregation in this area of employment. A respondent from an LGBT community organisation in Hastings drew attention to the particular problems faced by teachers who identify as gay or lesbian and confirmed that some of their members were adversely affected by the prevalence of negative attitudes in the school environment. She cited the example of one group member, who had come out as a lesbian, but lacked the confidence to be open about her sexuality at work as she "couldn't risk being seen by the pupils, for example going to gay social events".

The particular employment barriers faced by transgender people were also raised during interviews. As one respondent pointed out, the transgender population is estimated to be only about 1 in 10,000 of the population and this has made campaigning around 'trans' issues difficult:

> 'Transgender issues only came into the public consciousness in the late 1990s ... it's easy to not be visible and not be counted ... this can lead to high levels of stress, hostility and persecution ... people who look very different can be shunned, not employed and treated very badly.' (Female equalities worker, Brighton)

This point was reinforced by anecdotal evidence from a respondent in Hastings who recounted the hostility encountered at work by a transgender friend. She had delivered services to businesses in the retail trade but, following transition, found that some clients refused to work with her and "some shops wouldn't even allow her onto the premises to do her work" (female community activist, Hastings).

These accounts confirm the deeply embedded nature of homophobia and transphobia in the labour market and workplaces and reinforce arguments that the recent legislation outlawing discrimination on grounds of sexual orientation and gender identity can only be the beginnings of a solution. More fundamental social and cultural changes are required if full equality is to be achieved.

Conclusion: towards a broader approach

This chapter has argued that issues of sexual orientation and equality in employment are just one aspect of the wider discrimination and homophobia faced by LGBT people. Campaigns for sexual orientation equality in the labour market and the workplace are a continuation of the long-standing struggle by lesbians and gay men for political, social and legal rights. LGBT community organisations, more recently in the forefront of campaigning, have argued that the marginalisation – and frequent invisibility – of sexual orientation within equalities discourses has been reinforced by a rigid equalities infrastructure that has tended to create 'hierarchies of disadvantage' and the privileging of some dimensions of equality over others. The traditional equalities framework has also failed to adequately address the multidimensional nature of discrimination that many individuals and communities face.

The SEQUAL case studies have highlighted the factors that influence the labour market experiences of LGBT people including geographical context, health, poverty and social exclusion, and homophobic attitudes in the workplace. They have illustrated how discrimination linked to sexual orientation can have a significant impact, even in an apparently 'gay friendly' area such as Brighton & Hove, despite increasing official recognition of the distinctive contribution of the LGBT community to economic and cultural life. While the high profile of the Brighton gay scene was viewed as a positive affirmation of LGBT identity, there were also concerns that a narrow, stereotyped view of the LGBT population was failing to take account of its diversity and of the need for more robust and responsive equalities strategies to tackle discrimination and exclusion.

The research has also provided evidence of 'promising practices' among local LGBT community organisations in enhancing employability within wider strategies to tackle issues of social exclusion among vulnerable members of the LGBT community. In both localities, community organisations were offering holistic forms of support, combining employment training with the provision of 'safe spaces' for LGBT clients, which did not appear to be available in mainstream training programmes. Despite recent anti-discrimination legislation and the spread of a more 'enlightened' approach towards sexual orientation issues, the research also highlighted the deeply ingrained nature of homophobia in the workplace. It could be argued that the resulting inhibiting effects on personal identity and self-expression place many LGBT employees at a disadvantage within a labour market that increasingly emphasises the importance of interpersonal and communication skills within the workplace setting.

Many gay rights activists view the new Equality and Human Rights Commission (EHRC) as a potentially more effective instrument for promoting social justice than the traditional equalities framework from which they feel excluded (Stonewall, 2004). The establishment of a holistic human rights framework, which incorporated access to training and the labour market, as well as individualised political and civil rights as elaborated in Chapter Eleven later, would provide a more effective instrument for addressing complex dimensions of discrimination, including those relating to sexual orientation.

References

Bellis, A., Boice, M., Cairns, T. and McGrath, S. (2005) *In or out? Sexual orientation and the employability agenda: final report for the SEQUAL Development Partnership*, Guildford: SEQUAL Development Partnership, University of Surrey.

Brighton & Hove City Council Economic Development Team (2004) *Setting the scene: A review of the Brighton & Hove economy*, Brighton: Brighton & Hove City Council (www.brighton-hove.gov.uk/ business).

Brighton Ourstory Project (2001) *A history of Brighton's lesbian and gay community*, Brighton: Ourstory (www.brightonourstory.co.uk/lgbt. html).

Fairley, A. and Nouidjem, N. (2004) *Go Hastings!: Report of findings from research into the gay, lesbian, bisexual and transgendered community in Hastings and St Leonards, East Sussex*, Hastings: Rainbow Alliance.

LAGER (Lesbian and Gay Employment Rights) (2002) *A response to the consultation document 'Towards equality and diversity: Implementing the employment and race directives'*, London: LAGER.

McQuaid, R.W., Green, A. and Danson, M. (2005) 'Introducing employability', *Urban Studies*, vol 42, no 2, pp 191-5, February.

Morgan, L. and Bell, N. (2003) *First out: Report of the findings of the 'Beyond Barriers' national survey of LGBT people in Scotland*, Glasgow: Beyond Barriers/FMR Research Ltd.

New Economics Foundation (2005) *Coasting along: A study of business impacts and regeneration in south east coastal towns*, London: NEF (www.seeda.co.uk/Publications/Social_Inclusion/docs/ CoastalTownsOct2005.pdf).

Palmer, A. (1993) *'Less equal than others': A survey of lesbians and gay men at work*, London: Stonewall.

Palmer, A. (1995) 'Lesbian and gay rights campaigning: a report from the coalface', in A. Wilson (ed) *A simple matter of justice? Theorizing lesbian and gay politics*, London: Cassell, pp 32-50.

Stonewall (2004) *Fairness for all: A new Commission for Equality and Human Rights*, London: Stonewall.

Stonewall Cymru (2004) *Count us in!: Addressing the needs of Wales' forgotten 'community of interest'*, Cardiff: Stonewall Cymru (www. stonewall.org.uk/documents/Full_report_English.pdf).

Webb, D. and Wright, D. (2001) *Count me in: Findings from the lesbian, gay, bisexual, transgender community needs assessment 2000*, Brighton & Hove City Council.

Weeks, J. (1990) *Coming out: Homosexual politics in Britain from the nineteenth century to the present*, London: Quartet Books.

SEVEN

Youth discrimination and labour market access: from transitions to capabilities?

Mick Carpenter and Belinda Freda

Introduction: youth discrimination, still invisible after all these years

This chapter reviews young people's experience of the labour market, drawing on research for the SEQUAL project into a small group of Connexions clients. It explores their understandings and priorities, and then links this to wider evidence of labour market processes that impact on young people. A key feature of this is the way in which young people are socially constructed as being problematic and not just as having problems, which needs some prior discussion.

The SEQUAL research was conducted before significant measures to combat age discrimination in employment came into force as a result of the 2006 Employment Equality (Age) Regulations in the wake of the European Union's (EU's) 2000 Employment Framework Directive. The government also defends some 'age and experience' requirements as 'objectively justified', as well as lower National Minimum Wage (NMW) rates than the adult rate (Elliot, 2006). Protection on the grounds of age exists under the 1998 Human Rights Act, which prohibits discrimination on 'any grounds such as sex, race, colour, language, religion, political opinion, national or social origin, association with a national minority, property, birth or *other status*' (emphasis added). However, outside employment, there is no explicit legal protection against age discrimination. In this sphere too much of the media and public discussion has focused on discrimination of older workers. Our analysis of the government's Age Positive website (www.agepositive.gov.uk) in October 2006 showed that most of the 36 case studies of Age Positive Employer Champions, many leading public and private employers, focus chiefly on what employers are doing to recruit and retain older employers. If youth is mentioned, it is usually in terms of taking an 'age neutral' approach, although in the case of the Nationwide Building Society, younger employees are negatively associated with higher turnover by comparison with older ones. Most of the biographical examples given are of older workers.

In this chapter therefore we focus explicitly on 'youth' discrimination and equality as an issue in danger of being sidelined within age equality debates, and 'youth' discourses as often inherently discriminatory. Claims often previously made that young people are largely invisible, until identified as a problem or threat (for example, Davies, 1986), are still sustainable. The notion that 'youth' *is* a problem, an uncertain transition, not least in a rapidly changing 'knowledge' economy, rather than that young people sometimes *have* problems, lies at the heart of discriminatory processes, with varying class, 'race' and gender, and now religious sub-themes. There is a need to have a broader and more holistic view of the experience of young people if better solutions are to be developed, particularly in the light of the recent UNICEF report on children and young people where on a range of indicators Britain came bottom of the league of 21 leading industrialised countries (Adamson, 2007).

Our analysis therefore challenges government policy discourses (for example, SEU, 2005), which view youth as a uniquely 'transitional' social status. Instead we see it as a set of socially variable experiences, rather than defined in terms of a socially prescribed 'adult' destination. As the boundaries between various stages of life become blurred, factors such as extended family dependence, growth of higher education and postponed childbearing further call into question the viability of describing youth as a brief transition. Rather than extending the boundaries of youth, we need to revise standard ideas of what it means to be 'adult'. What happens to young people's rights is potentially of wider interest. Thus the erosion of human and social rights that occurred initially in relation to the New Deal for Young People (NDYP) through mandatory participation in work or training is, as other chapters in this book illustrate, by stages being extended to others through 'welfare reform' – lone parents, older workers and disabled people – as part of a wider shift to a workfare state.

The relatively low levels of ILO (International Labour Organization) unemployment among young people in Britain since the 1990s, compared with some other European countries, and its 'containment' by NDYP has led to a diminished concern with youth unemployment, and, by extension, interest and concern about the quality of young people's experience in the labour market. However, rates of unemployment are higher among young people than other age groups, and are particularly high among some minority ethnic groups. Additionally, there is evidence that young people are generally under intense pressure in the 'new economy'. While this falls heaviest on the most vulnerable, life is often 'hard' for many young people beyond the age of 16, as the SEQUAL research illustrates.

Labour market experiences: finding a place in a hard world

One feature of the Surrey SEQUAL research into young people involved the testing out of a small-scale intensive approach to exploring the experiences and needs of young people in the labour market, giving prominence to their own voices and the views of experienced youth workers. Using qualitative and collaborative methods, it piloted a promising practice for obtaining insights and also generating policy proposals. Five young people from a range of backgrounds volunteered to take part after the research was explained to, and then 'promoted' by, youth workers in local youth clubs and Connexions centres. The young people gave up their time freely to talk to the researcher and did not receive any financial incentive. They were tracked over a period of 18 months, and an advisory panel of four experienced youth workers was also formed. The primary aim was to understand issues, such as employment choices, employability skills in today's labour market, role of youth agencies, and experience of discrimination from the perspective of young people themselves and also of youth workers who individually acted as expert advisers.

All the young people were in some form of post-school education or training, but not particularly 'advantaged' in the labour market per se. Alice was a young Black woman from a single-parent background, her mother remarrying in 2003. She was doing a GNVQ in Health and Social Care with a view to doing a childminding course. Her longer-term plan was to study child psychology at university. Mary, with a dual heritage, was also from a single-parent background and was taking the same course, but unsure about higher education. Jane, a refugee from Kosovo, was taking 'A' levels with a view to studying pharmacology at university. Steve was a White young man who was experiencing health and emotional difficulties and had been diagnosed with epilepsy three years previously. He had started an IT (information technology) diploma and a Business Studies course but dropped the latter, as he felt there was insufficient support at school. John was a White male, whose father had died at an early age and had been brought up by his mother. When interviewed in 2004 he was starting a BSc in

International Relations, and was extremely concerned about student loans. Informal meetings with the young people took place every two months over the 18-month period, in locations such as fast food outlets and parks, and regular contact maintained by email, text message and phone calls. The expert advisers were a Connexions personal adviser, two managers of advice and guidance projects and an experienced independent consultant.

All the young people in the study, with the exception of Steve, had clear ideas of what they wanted to do and going to university figured highly for most. The young people put a lot of research and effort into finding out what qualifications and skills were required for their field of interest, and what opportunities existed. Our small group also showed expected gender differences, choosing 'feminised' and 'masculinised' educational routes to careers. They were thus taking considerable steps to enhance their 'employability'. For most, 'interest' in their career was what motivated them most, as well as security. In the case of pharmacology Jane said "people will always need medicine"; Mary said "people will always have kids"; and Steve believed that IT was a secure sector. A number chose routes that offered possibilities of travel after qualification or graduation. Young men like John were particularly likely to see higher education as a necessary but uncertain "investment", which taking out a loan reinforced, "but I am not sure it will be immediately worth it".

All regarded the labour market as a hard, competitive place, and had realistic views of what they needed to do in order to fit into it. There was little sense in the interviews about youth being a carefree time of life. Some embraced this world enthusiastically. Jane, from a refugee background, described herself as a "terrier ... I can't wait to get in there!", and felt that the labour market offered "work for everyone. If you want to work, everyone has his or her place and there's a place for everyone". Others were not so sure. Alice thought that "you have to look after No 1", and Mary said "you have to work longer these days".

Health shaped strategies and possibilities for some of the young people. While Mary had been forced to change childcare courses as a result of health difficulties, she nevertheless remained on track. However, Steve had been forced to lower his aspirations by dropping one of his courses after he had been diagnosed with epilepsy. He stated that he found it hard to concentrate and had "a bad memory". He was concerned about what potential employers and work colleagues might think:

'You can't see it so I might just lie. I don't want to be treated differently.'

The young people also talked about the factors that influenced their choices. Mary and Jane felt they had chosen their pathways as they "adore" children, but had also received much support and advice from their Connexions adviser and parents. Jane was strongly influenced by her parents' desire for her to get a secure and professional job, which is why she chose pharmacology, despite her greater interest in the media. Both Steve and John were strongly influenced by their parents. Mary felt that 'peer pressure' shaped young people's choices generally:

'A lot of my friends just started courses in beauty therapy because their mates were doing it and then they dropped out. They're just not thinking ahead.'

The three young women all felt this might be alleviated if more options were made available.

When asked their perceptions about which 'employability' attributes employers were looking for, there was agreement that these were generic skills. They particularly mentioned general issues of motivation and the kinds of 'soft' skills that are particularly associated with an individualist and post-industrial labour market. Much of service work is also increasingly 'aesthetic' work where smart appearance and presentation, and youthfulness, are part of the commodified personal relations in service labour (Nickson et al, 2004). This was most frequently summed up as being 'responsible for yourself', to which 'responsibility to others' was sometimes added. This notion of self-direction was partly focused on the needs of employers but also, discussed later in this chapter, linked to the common aspiration towards 'autonomy'. The other most mentioned attributes were communication and interpersonal skills. Humour and resilience was mentioned by Alice, while resourcefulness was mentioned by both young men and women. Two of the young women and one of the young men mentioned appearance as an important asset. Both Jane and John mentioned 'quick thinking'. There was very little mention of hard skills such as literacy, numeracy or familiarity with IT but 'qualifications' were mentioned. Young people's comments were largely echoed by the expert advisers, the only difference being that they were more likely to mention relevant experience, confidence and esteem and team working. On the whole, then, they too mentioned the importance of soft skills, and mentioned training courses like the Prince's Trust Personal 12-step Development

Programme as an example of good practice. Motivation was seen as fundamental, as "you've got to get the platform right, a positive attitude, and then go on to practical job-search skills".

The Social Exclusion Unit (2005) report on young adults with complex needs also emphasised changing 'thinking and behaviour' as the necessary step before skills acquisition. They put considerable emphasis on preparing young people for the 'realities' of the labour market, echoing the comments of the young people. As one put it, Thatcherism had left people reliant on their own wits to survive and progress. These perceptions of the labour market connect to the concept of 'risk society' and notions of individualisation as advanced by Beck (1992). Both the young people and the youth workers seemed to see this as a fixed part of the economic landscape, rather than as anything that can be challenged. The removal of public safety nets has arguably prolonged dependence of many young people on parents (for example, Coles, 1995), as some of the respondents confirmed, which may not be available to the most vulnerable, including those leaving care (SEU, 2005). If the expert advisers criticised the official 'employability' discourse, it was only at the edges, for example, "the country's obsession with getting 50% of young people into higher education".

The young people all claimed to have experienced age discrimination. Jane had also experienced prejudice and stereotyping as a result of her refugee status and being Kosovan. A number had experienced disability discrimination directly or indirectly through relatives, as in Steve's case. They expressed support for a 'social' rather than 'medical' model, seeing the prime problems as due to "very unfriendly" environments, and employers reluctant to invest in disabled employees. Where discrimination by sexual orientation occurred, it was seen as more likely to come from work colleagues than employers in the guise of bullying and teasing. The expert advisers echoed the young people's views on disability, and complained that employers were proactive in tackling harassment and bullying associated with homophobia, racism and other forms of discrimination in the workplace. There were a number of critical comments that young people received a lower NMW, which in any case was often flouted, and had negative effects on those who needed to live independently, like those leaving care.

Youth workers felt that young people with mental health problems were especially likely to experience employment discrimination. In 2004 it was estimated that 12.6% of boys and 10.3% of girls aged 11-16 had a 'clinically diagnosable' disorder. Boys in particular were most likely to experience behaviour and hyperkinetic problems. Rates were higher in lone and 'reconstituted' families, and where parents had few or no qualifications (Green et al, 2004, pp 8-9). In other words, mental health difficulties magnify other social disadvantages. A study by Stephens (2002) found that mental health problems, and physical disabilities, were both a cause and consequence of homelessness and magnified the risk of labour market exclusion. Young men are more at risk than young women, and around one third of homeless young people have been in care.

There is currently only limited evidence about young people's experience of discrimination in the UK labour market. A YouGov survey of 1,300 people in employment conducted for Royal and SunAlliance in May 2006 revealed that 14% of young workers felt their progression had been hindered because of age, compared to 10% of people over the age of 45. They point out that companies need to balance the need to provide progression opportunities for young people, while accommodating older workers. Where age legislation exists, as in the US and Ireland, it has become a strong focus for litigation and tribunal cases ('News Release', 8 August 2006, www.royalsunalliance. com). Research commissioned by the former Department for Education and Employment, conducted among 114 young people aged 16-30 in early 2001, did not seek to make an assessment of the extent of discrimination but did ascertain that complaints of it were common while being difficult to prove. Much of it occurred through 'coded' recruitment literature. While qualifications did not necessarily open doors, those without them were most likely to raise complaints of discrimination. Entrants in established professions like law and accountancy were the most likely graduates to complain about discrimination. Where younger people were seen to be at an advantage in the labour market, it was only because they were cheaper to employ. Some had been told they had failed interviews because they were too young. Discrimination could consist of inappropriate behaviour such as teasing or being patronised. Overall the report found that a range of contextual issues shaped the likelihood of discrimination against young people, including demand factors such as levels of unemployment, and replaceability or need to retain staff, and cultural factors such as whether a firm or employment setting was traditional and hierarchical or 'modern' and flexible (Andrew Irving Associates, 2001).

In talking about discrimination, the young people in our small-scale study identified a range of difficulties, not all of which are exclusive to young people:

• difficulty in obtaining a good entry-level job, in the absence of skills, qualifications and/or experience;

- negative stereotyping of young people as "yobbish", unreliable, scruffy, and lacking communication skills;
- given "crap jobs" with little skill content and lack of access to training to develop them;
- discrimination against newcomers of any age in relation to employment policies such as redundancy procedures;
- lack of opportunities to exercise responsibility or positive feedback about work well done. "Being valued" as a person and employee rather than being treated as a disposable resource was mentioned often as an important motivating factor;
- either the current generation is seen as "lucky and spoilt" and expecting progress without effort, or as "pushy" if they do show ambition. Thus whatever they do is seen in a negative light.

This chimes with the limited wider evidence on employment discrimination among young people. Application forms and many job specifications focus on chronology and career time-lines rather than on competency and ability. These do not just discriminate against young people, but also those with interrupted career paths, whether due to caring responsibilities, travel, ill health or other reasons, such as being in prison. Some progress has been made and alternative resources and methods exist. The Employers' Forum on Age has promoted age-neutral application forms (Employers' Forum on Age, 2006).

Autonomy, the youth labour market and human rights

The desire for autonomy emerged as an important issue in the SEQUAL research and in other European and UK consultations with young people, for example, the European Youth Forums (www.youthforum. org). Among the young people tracked in this research 'autonomy' was viewed as independence (financial and in general), being respected by others (adults), and ultimately having the freedom to make genuine choices. Not surprisingly perhaps, money was mentioned by all young people as something that would "empower" them. 'Autonomy' touches on all aspects of life, not just employment.

The relation of government policies to youth autonomy are highly inconsistent, indicating widespread uncertainty about when one ceases to be a child and becomes an adult. The movement to the Youth Training Scheme (YTS) in the mid-1980s removed rights to social security from those aged 16-18 and the New Deals have further limited young people's choices in relation to independent living and choices with regard to employment. The low level of NMW rates has already been identified and there are a myriad of other discriminatory age distinctions, for example, relating to Housing Benefit and tax credits (Calder, 2004). These policies extend youth transitions and are arguably an abuse of human rights. ILO unemployment statistics define someone as a young person if they are aged under 25.

Australia has introduced a single although means-tested Youth Allowance with the aim of ensuring that eligible young people receive adequate financial support while studying and looking and preparing for paid work. It is available from the age of 16. The maximum age is 25 years for full-time students and 21 for other young people (www. dest.gov.au). It aims to aid school retention and encourage young people to stay in further education. It has been advocated for the UK and, although promising, there are some potential lessons, in that the criteria that determine 'dependent' or 'independent' status are blurred and complex and it is paid to parents in the case of most under-18-year-olds. The majority of recipients are students rather than jobseekers, with a tendency for the most disadvantaged or socially marginalised not to apply, such as the homeless or those with mental health problems. There were uncertainties about whether young lone parents or carers could combine their responsibilities with part-time education or job search activities (Finn and Branosky, 2004).

From a human rights perspective, while designating any age as the start of adulthood is bound to be arbitrary, consistency would seem the fairest approach. The 'age of majority' implies a concept of autonomy by referring to the legal age at which people can be deemed to direct their own life and financial affairs, enter into contracts, vote and so on, and our argument is that this should provide the key statutory benchmark. In the UK this is currently set at 18, although there is a case for lowering it to 16 years. There is therefore a politically available single threshold age at which people could be positively regarded as having adult 'capabilities' in Sen's (1999) sense. In arguing this, we draw on Jeffs and Smith (1998/99, p 45), who argue, '"youth" has limited use as a social category and it characteristically involves viewing those so named as being in deficit and in need of training and control'.

Mizen argues that the transitional view of youth is a top-down 'political construction' by policy makers seeking to set predetermined stages through which young people are expected to pass (Mizen, 2002). He argues that the wider context in which this has occurred is a shift from a Keynesian to a neoliberal state, in which young people are increasingly compelled to acquire more employability traits, from school years onwards, and bear the financial costs in terms of restricted benefits and student loans.

While this system makes life generally hard for young people, it bears particularly heavily on those who become most socially excluded by it, who are then blamed by government policy discourses, aided by sections of the media. Thus policy attention has shifted from ILO unemployment to the group of young people post-16 who are defined as 'not in education, employment or training' or 'NEETs'. The Youth Cohort Study showed that overall the proportion of 16- to 18-year-olds in education and training was 76.2% at the end of 2005, at 1.5 million the highest number ever (ONS, 2006). This was subject to social variations, by class, ethnicity and gender (Babb et al, 2006, p 39). In terms of ethnicity, all groups were improving their attainment of 5 or more GCSE grades A–C. However, Asians, with the exception of Bangladeshis, were improving performance to a greater extent than White, although Black young people's educational attainment had improved the least, particularly among boys. Young women substantially outperform young men up to 'A' levels and beyond, in virtually all ethnic groups (Babb et al, 2006, pp 41-2; DfES, 2006).

Government policy discourses focus on the supply side. The fact that those who leave school without qualifications have a tough future ahead of them is often presumed to be due to the needs of a 'knowledge' economy, rather than deprivation and disadvantage and alterable demand-side factors (DfES, 2006). Yet there remains a mismatch between the generally higher educational attainment of young women and many minority ethnic groups and their labour market chances. In the spring of 2006, minority ethnic groups generally experienced an ILO unemployment rate of 11.2% compared with 5.2% overall, 0.9% higher than a year previously, and an economic inactivity rate of 32.8% compared with 21.2% overall (EMED, 2006). While the government proclaims the success of NDYP programmes, those who go through them often experience 'churning', that is, they do not permanently exit the scheme (Finn, 2003; Worth, 2005). So-called NEETs are not reached at all, even though many policies such as the youth service Connexions have been targeted in their direction. This group of young people have become the new focus for discriminatory moral panics and demonisation by statistics, as in a *Sunday Times* article that described them as an 'underclass timebomb':

> A study by the DfES conservatively estimates that each new NEET dropping out will cost taxpayers an average of £97,000 during their lifetime, with the worst costing

more than £300,000 apiece. Their impact on crime, public
health and anti-social behaviour was so marked that the
study found that a single 157,000-strong cohort of 16 to
18-year-old NEETS would cost the country a total of £15
billion by the time they died prematurely in about 2060.
(Winnett, 2005)

Around 12% of young people in 2005 were in this category, the
number remaining relatively stable over the previous decade (ONS,
2006). Without ignoring the role played by young people's personal
choices, there is need for a more structural explanation in the way that
a polarised hourglass economy, discussed in more detail in Chapters
Ten and Eleven later, impacts on young people.

What is lacking in much public discussion to date is a recognition
that the supply-side 'work-first' approach associated with NDYP may
be part of the problem. Conservative commentators like Worth (2005)
argue for a stronger skills element to meet the skills gap, rather than
simply integrating young people into low-paid work. This does not
take account, however, of the fact that significant numbers of young
people with multiple disadvantages are not 'work ready', as pointed out
by the Social Exclusion Unit (SEU, 2005), who advocate personalised
support and training based on notions of 'distance travelled'. This
model is influenced by youth transition theory and we would argue
for focusing it more broadly on 'capabilities' than predetermined
journey destinations. As Yates and Payne (2006) argue, the NEET
category defines young people in terms of a presumed deficit and
fails to take account of their heterogeneous circumstances. They
argue that this encourages a firefighting approach by the Connexions
service seeking to meet demanding targets to reduce the numbers
of NEETs, preventing them from taking a holistic, person-centred
approach. Cisse (2000) has also expressed some doubts concerning the
Connexions personal adviser system. Despite its undoubted strengths,
it individualises solutions that may have collective causes, shifting
attention away from the need to transform the wider structures of
power that disadvantage young people.

As well as improved 'supply-side' approaches, these issues draw
attention to the need to focus more on the demand side. Worth (2005)
recognises this by showing that while the image of insecurity in the
labour force is generally overdrawn, young people are the group most
likely to experience it, particularly those with few, if any, qualifications.
Unfortunately, however, he does not call for stronger demand-side
interventions to raise wages and force improvements in skill levels and

management practices that can be justified on both human rights and economic grounds, as elaborated in Chapter Eleven later.

Conclusion: young people as social assets with lives of their own

Our small-scale research with young people and youth workers focused primarily on the perceptions of a group who were relatively diverse and, although suffering disadvantages, were striving hard to advance their higher education and employment in a difficult world. They were not among the most disadvantaged, but they were acutely aware of discriminatory processes, although this had not discouraged them. Their views corresponded closely to those of the expert advisers and also to the limited wider evidence that exists on the employment discrimination of young people. The research indicated that although they wanted to advance their education and career, their central concern was to establish their autonomy as self-directed and 'capable' adults. This approach implicitly challenges the 'problem'- and 'transition'-focused approach that informs much policy and practice, including that advocated by the Social Exclusion Unit in its policy work on disadvantaged young people. The small numbers mean that they cannot be regarded as representative, but their actions correspond to the increasing numbers of young people who are seeking to advance their prospects by undertaking post-16 training and education. Wider evidence also broadly supports the conclusions that were reached.

The method that we have developed on a small scale in this chapter has potential for a more widespread participative approach drawing on the experiences and insights of young people and youth workers, which can be compared with and contrasted to the assumptions of government policies and the wider research evidence. Taking a human rights approach based on capabilities, with a central focus on autonomy as a key objective, therefore implies that the concept of youth as a variable transition into rights and responsibilities is inherently discriminatory, and calls into question the imposition of costs and compulsions. Thus, rather than facilitating autonomy and participation, policies operating in discriminatory ways may therefore help to exacerbate social exclusion and disengagement.

References

Adamson, P. (2007) *Child poverty in perspective: An overview of child well-being in rich countries*, Florence: UNICEF, Report card 7.

Andrew Irving Associates (2001) *Ageism: Attitudes and expenses of young people*, London: Department for Work and Pensions.

Babb, P., Butcher, H., Church, J. and Zealey, L. (2006) *Social trends 36*, London: Office for National Statistics.

Beck, U. (1992) *Risk society: Towards a new modernity*, London: Sage Publications.

Calder, A. (2004) 'Young people and benefits', *Benefits*, vol 40, no 2, pp 129-31.

Cisse, T. (2000) *Beyond Connexions – Issues in constructive engagement*, Infed: the Informal Education Encyclopaedia (www.infed.org/personaladvisers/cisse-connexions.htm).

Coles, B. (1995) *Youth and social policy: Youth citizenship and youth careers*, London: UCL Press.

Davies, B. (1986) *Threatening youth: Towards a national youth policy*, Milton Keynes: Open University Press.

DfES (Department for Education and Skills) (2006) *Ethnicity and education: The evidence on minority ethnic pupils aged 5-16*, Research topic paper, London: DfES.

Elliot, L. (2006) 'New ageism laws may spark minimum wage challenge', *The Guardian*, 30 September.

Employers' Forum on Age (2006) 'Study digs up golden nuggets', *Working Age*, Autumn, p 3 (www.efa.org.uk/publications/downloads/Working-Age-Issue6.pdf).

EMED (Ethnic Minority Employment Division) (2006) *Ethnic minorities in the labour market: Spring 2006*, EME Division, Department for Work and Pensions (www.emetaskforce.gov.uk/reports.asp).

Finn, D. (2003) 'The "employment-first" welfare state: lessons from the New Deal for Young People', *Social Policy and Administration*, vol 37, no 7, pp 709-24.

Finn, D. and Branosky, N. (2004) *Financial support for 16 to 19 year olds: A review of the literature and evidence on the Australian Youth Allowance*, DWP Research Report No 215, London: Department for Work and Pensions.

Green, H., McGinty, A., Meltzer, H., Ford, T. and Goodman, R. (2004) *Mental health of children and young people in Great Britain, 2004: Summary report*, London: Department of Health.

Jeffs, T. and Smith, M.K. (1998/99) 'The problem of "youth" for youth work', *Youth and Policy*, no 62, Winter, pp 45-66.

Mizen, P. (2002) 'Putting the politics back into youth studies: Keynesianism, monetarism and the changing state of youth', *Journal of Youth Studies*, vol 5, no 1, pp 5-20.

Nickson, D., Warhurst, C. and Dutton, E. (2004) *Aesthetic labour and the policy-making agenda: Time for a reappraisal of skills*, SKOPE Research Paper No 48, Glasgow: Scottish Centre for Employment Research.

ONS (Office for National Statistics) (2006) *Participation in education, training and employment by 16-18 year olds in England: 2004 and 2005*, London: ONS (www.statistics.gov.uk).

Sen, A. (1999) *Development as freedom*, Oxford: Oxford University Press.

SEU (Social Exclusion Unit) (2005) *Transitions: Young people with complex needs. A Social Exclusion Unit final report*, London: Office of the Deputy Prime Minister.

Stephens, J. (2002) *The mental health needs of homeless young people. Bright futures: Working with vulnerable young people*, London: Mental Health Foundation.

Winnett, R. (2005) 'Meet the NEETS: a new underclass', *The Sunday Times*, 27 March (www.timesonline.co.uk/tol/news/uk/article438356. ece).

Worth, S. (2005) 'Beating the "churning" trap in the youth labour market', *Work, Employment and Society*, vol 19, no 2, pp 403-14.

Yates, S. and Payne, M. (2006) 'Not so NEET? A critique of the use of "NEET" in setting targets for interventions with young people', *Journal of Youth Studies*, vol 9, no 3, pp 329-44.

EIGHT

Employability in the third age: a qualitative study of older people in the Glasgow labour market

Pamela Clayton

Introduction

This chapter, like the preceding one on youth, focuses on equality issues related to age. It proceeds by first highlighting the significance of age discrimination in the context of it often being considered socially less important than racism, sexism or other forms of oppression. It is argued that the concept of the 'third age' is potentially a basis from which to challenge age oppression, as long as diversity issues are taken into account. Recent trends in discrimination and human rights policies and their benefits and limitations for older people are then reviewed, before the chapter focuses centrally on the SEQUAL research into a group of older adult learners that sought to highlight their experiences in the labour market and give voice to their views about them.

Diversity and discrimination in third age experiences

The anti-ageist term 'third age' seeks to combat the stereotyping of old age as a time of necessary withdrawal and disengagement from social life, followed by inevitable physical and mental decline. The third age refers to the stage in life at which people may be moving towards the close of their full-time working careers while remaining active and independent. The concept originated in France in 1972 and was introduced in Britain through the self-help leisure and educational organisation University of the Third Age (U3A) in 1981 (www.u3a-info.co.uk). The concept does not imply a specific age, as the age at which people are considered 'old' varies greatly, according to sector, class, gender or ethnicity. In some spheres, such as computer engineering, 35 may be considered old, while in politics or the judiciary 60 may be thought young. Thus while 45-50 is a commonly used boundary between the second and third ages, entry to it is variable (Plant, 2005).

For policy research purposes some boundary has to be set, and there is also a need to differentiate phases within 'old age'. Rather than taking the state pension age as the boundary, the Family and Working Lives Survey on the employment and family histories of a sample of around 11,000 people decided on 50 as a threshold: this is the age at which manual workers' risk of long-term unemployment rises (McKay and Middleton, 1998). The English Longitudinal Study of Ageing (ELSA) chose the same point at which to review the health experiences of older people when differences in class mortality, especially among men, become apparent (IFS, 2006). These studies and other research also reveal considerable diversity among older people in terms of social identities and experiences such as gender, class, sexuality, health, residence and skills, as well as aspirations, interests and family situation (Loretto et al, 2006).

The emerging evidence in this under-researched area is that ageism is a widespread general experience compounded by other forms of social disadvantage and discrimination. A 2006 representative survey of people aged 16 to over 75 conducted for Age Concern England revealed that age discrimination was the commonest form of reported discrimination – reported by 28% in the past year – followed by gender, 'race' or ethnicity, religion, disability and sexual orientation. People over 70 tend to be regarded favourably but as incompetent, while young people under 30 are regarded as more competent but are less likely to be viewed favourably, indicating that ageism is a single binary phenomenon. The study thought that there might be under-reporting by older people, on the basis that "it's only natural". Despite its prevalence, however, age discrimination is regarded as less serious than other forms, again particularly among older people (Ray et al, 2006, pp 47-9).

In terms of labour market experiences, the long-term trend has been towards earlier retirement, described by one qualitative study as 'pull or push' (Irving et al, 2005), which could be reframed sociologically in terms of 'structure and agency'. Strong push factors were redundancy, serious ill health and prescribed retirement ages. Pull factors depended on whether or not people had sufficient financial security to enter, whether partially or fully, the 'third age'. Vickerstaff (2006) has argued that too much emphasis has been given to individual supply-side agency, as opposed to demand-side pressures transmitted through employers. Her case study research found that workers often regarded compulsory retirement as unfair, although those on low incomes felt compelled to continue even though they would rather 'downsize' or retire. Much of this was conditioned during the Thatcher years by deindustrialisation and high unemployment, in which older working people were expected by employers, the government and trade unions to 'make way' for younger working people. The trend in recent years has been in the opposite direction, due to economic recovery and labour shortages. Trade unions have become more aware of broader discrimination issues, older people have been asserting their rights more and governments have been seeking to encourage older workers to stay in or re-enter the labour force because of concerns about an impending 'demographic crisis'. There has, therefore, been a mixed set of influences, involving a range of actors.

The result of all this has been a rise in the employment rate of older workers between the ages of 50 and 64. In the UK this rose from 65.2% in 1995 to 72.5% by 2004, faster among men than women, and almost 10% of people over 65 were in work, mainly part time (DWP, 2005a, pp 23-4). The government is seeking to raise this further by a number of measures that seek both to persuade and cajole older people in varying degrees, although the latter approach tends to be downplayed. The Green Paper on welfare reform (DWP, 2006), which is discussed further in Chapter Ten, talks positively of 'empowering' and 'helping' older workers, and sets a target of one million extra workers, linked to raising women's state pension age to 65 between 2010 and 2020.

The shifting balance between rights and responsibilities for older workers

On the plus side, prodded by the European Union's (EU's) 2000 Framework Directive, in late 2006 the government introduced the Employment Equality (Age) Regulations that provide better protection against age discrimination in employment and vocational guidance and training – but not outside these spheres. Even within them, exceptions include 'a maximum recruitment age based on the training requirements of the post'. This perpetuates the stereotype of older people as less competent despite evidence that, although memory and processing speed start to decline from around the age of 35, people often become more competent in understanding and knowledge (Age Concern Policy Unit, 2004, p 22). The regulations outlaw harassment on grounds of age, age discrimination in recruitment and promotion and forced retirement below the age of 65, 'except where objectively justified'. They remove the grossly discriminatory upper age limit (65 for men and 60 for women) for unfair dismissal and redundancy rights. They also give all employees the 'right to request' working beyond retirement age, which employers must consider, although they can refuse without giving a reason (Lewis and Sargeant, 2007, chapter 7). The regulations thus continue to enshrine the discrimination involved in compulsory retirement or denying jobs on the grounds of age beyond retirement age.

This may well be tested under the 1998 Human Rights Act, the provisions of which are explained in more detail in Chapter Eleven. Although the Human Rights Act provides protection against discrimination it does this on civil and political grounds, rather than providing access to economic, social and cultural rights, such as access to work and social security. The government has developed a range of policies that seek to tempt workers into employment through options such as more generous provisions for people who delay taking their pensions.

The Age Positive Campaign is a means through which the Department for Work and Pensions promotes age diversity by means of positive policies to recruit and retain older workers, including provision of flexible approaches to part-time working, with the retail firm B&Q being the most frequently quoted example (www.agepositive.gov.uk). It argues this on the ground of the 'business case' of lower turnover and other benefits, which Chapter Seven argues is potentially prejudicial against young people. The government is taking two further steps that, while having some benefits, may also have a negative impact on some older people. First, it has accepted the recommendation of the Turner Commission on pensions reform to raise the state pension age in stages to 68 by 2050 (Pensions Commission, 2007). This may be discriminatory against disadvantaged working-class men, significant numbers of whom, as we shall see later in the context of Glasgow, may not live to collect a pension. Second, the shift to greater conditionality in welfare reform in the wake of the Green Paper (DWP, 2006) will have some negative consequences for older workers or claimants, enforcing rather than simply encouraging participation. Thus people aged between 50 and 59 will be required to take up additional 'jobseeking support', although they and their dependent partners over 50 will be eligible for improved back-to-work support. People over 50 will also be disproportionately affected by the replacement of Incapacity Benefit with the Employment Support Allowance due to be implemented in 2008, as highlighted in Chapter Three.

The broader context of welfare reform and alternatives to current policies are discussed in Chapters Ten and Eleven. The main emphasis is being placed on developing rights to real choices to enter the labour market on a full- or part-time basis and, if empowerment is genuinely the goal, enjoy a decent way of life outside it. Such changes are underpinned by an emphasis on enhancing the employability of those currently out of the labour market, which is focused on minimum criteria consistent with a work-first approach to integrating people into available jobs. This is followed by assumptions that one of the key problems is either low or unrealistic expectations and that there is a need to discipline people, including older workers, to take what is available. While the Green Paper recognises 'structural, personal and cultural barriers' for those who wish to continue working (DWP, 2006, p 62), the greatest emphasis is placed on the last two, leading to policies that seek to change people rather than wider circumstances. If the latter were considered, the needs of older people in the knowledge economy for reskilling or 'modern apprenticeships' might be considered. Instead, the implementation of the Treasury's Leitch Report (HM Treasury, 2006), discussed in Chapter Eleven, is likely to lead to an increased concentration on younger age groups. The government might also consider doing something more concerted about Britain's 'long hours' culture, and end the opt-out from the EU Working Time Directive (O'Neill, 2006). In other words, it can be argued that there needs to be more demand-side intervention to improve the quality of jobs rather than creating more conditional welfare-to-work that forces older and younger people into competition for undesirable and insecure employment.

Glasgow research in context

The issues raised in the first part of this chapter will now be linked to the SEQUAL research undertaken in Glasgow, a city of over 650,000 people, where over 40% of those between 50 and pension age were outside the labour market (The Scottish Government, 2006). Once famous as a great industrial city, where people found employment in shipbuilding, heavy engineering, mining, factory work and associated trades and services, it was also notable for poor housing and health and high rates of crime and violence. By the mid-1970s all but a fraction of its industry was gone and with it many skilled trades. Recession brought high levels of unemployment, from which the city has not completely recovered. Glasgow is also, however, a vibrant, beautiful city where many people today earn a good living in the service industries. The proportion of people assigned to Social Classes A and B has risen from less than 20% in 1981 to the Scottish average of almost 40%. Those who have not benefited from Glasgow's revival live in outlying areas of high, long-term unemployment, continuing poor health and poverty and worsening male life expectancy (Hanlon et al, 2006, chapter 4). Average male life expectancy in Glasgow is 69.1; but the range by area extends from 63.5 to 78.7, with the highest and lowest postcode sectors ranging from 53.9 to 82.6 (Hanlon et al, 2006, chapter 3). If this does not improve in the coming years, many working-class Glasgow men will not live to collect pensions when the retirement age is increased to 68.

The qualitative data presented is analysed from a survey of people in the Glasgow area who agreed to life-history interviews, recorded and transcribed verbatim, focusing on education and employment that took place between 1995 and 1998. The 105 people in the survey were adult learners selected by employers and a range of learning providers. There were 22 aged 50 or over, 10 of whom were out of the labour market, three were unemployed, two men were employed full time and seven women worked part-time. All respondents were White – Glasgow being a city with low numbers of Black and minority ethnic (BME) residents – and have been given fictitious names. The analysis here concentrates on the degree of choice they were able to exercise in staying in or leaving the labour market – in other words, the extent to which the interviewees enjoyed the dignity of autonomy, self-determination and a decent standard of living, consistent with a broad human rights approach, rather than constraint and poverty.

Barriers to employment

The SEQUAL analysis identified three main sets of barriers experienced by individuals in the study aged over 50 for obtaining, retaining or returning to employment. First, of the four people who suffered unemployment, lifetime disadvantage was compounded by age discrimination that affected their ability to access the labour market. All came from working-class families where working was reportedly 'the normal thing to do' and adhered strongly to the work ethic. Each had left school at the minimum leaving age. John and Robert entered skilled trades and Dorothy became a nurse, while Jim embarked on a series of unskilled and semi-skilled jobs, many of them casual. They were continuously employed until their forties, except for Dorothy, who spent just four years looking after her children full time and entered unemployment at the age of 55 when her unit was closed. All stated they were in good health but since the forced end of their careers, only John had worked again but did not secure a permanent job. All of them had work qualifications or had continued learning while unemployed. John had used his redundancy money to learn new skills and Robert had obtained a university degree.

Jim and Robert felt strongly that their age counted against them. Jim's last and longest-lasting job was as a plater in the shipyard, but "when you reach a certain age people don't want to employ you – the age barrier!". Nevertheless, he still felt that the confidence and skills he had gained through his voluntary work might lead to a job one day. Robert, however, after having many job applications ignored, had given up:

> 'I can't get a job at all.... They're not interested. I think it's
> – age has something to do with it but, having said that, I just
> – I've never even had an interview, not even the courtesy
> of.... You should still be able to find something ... it doesna
> matter, that's how it goes.'

He even identified with the employer's point of view:

> 'If I was an employer, somebody came in at 30 years of age
> and I came in – we both had the same – I mean, I wouldna
> employ me either, because whoever's 30 or whatever age
> you are, you're that wee bit quicker.'

Second, geographical mobility is much harder for older working-class people who have deep roots in their area and often lack the resources to move to an area with more jobs but also higher living costs. Thus none of the interviewees felt in a position to relocate.

Third, where only insecure low-wage jobs seem to be on offer, the loss of social security benefits acted as a strong deterrent. Liz, aged 58, decided not to go for a job because she felt that she would not be able to earn enough to compensate for the loss of benefits. She was used to living on very little and enjoyed doing voluntary work. Thus despite government efforts to 'make work pay', a number of respondents in the sample were reluctant at this stage in their life to gamble their benefits against low-paid work with few perceived prospects for promotion. They also weighed the costs involved, such as travel, appropriate clothing and lunches out.

Of course, not all vacancies are at the lower end of the pay scale. There is, for example, a serious shortage of electrical engineers in parts of the UK. In one study, however, very few employers with recruitment problems agreed that early retirement should be discouraged and it was unusual to find recruitment policies that included people aged over 45 (Spence and Kelly, 2003). So some well-paid jobs are effectively barred to older people.

These problems are compounded by other inequality issues that affect all age groups, such as class (including 'postcode discrimination'), gender, ethnicity and the psychological effects of absence from the labour market. Particular factors affect people over 50 disproportionately, such as health and disability and lack of qualifications. In the 50 to retirement age group, 21.8% have no formal qualifications, compared with only 6.3% of those aged 16-24 and 7% of those aged 25-49 (DWP, 2005b). Good health is an important issue for many employers: working-class people in particular are more likely to experience deteriorating health after 50 (IFS, 2006). Thus, many older unemployed people or returners may not be instantly 'employable'. There is considerable evidence that inequalities in health impact strongly on Glasgow, as a city with some of the worst ill health in the UK. This seems to be due to the combined effects of class disadvantage linked to poverty and unemployment and the stress resulting from a changing labour market and industrial base, which may compound lifestyle influences linked to smoking, alcohol and a diet high in saturated fat (Scottish Executive, 2003).

Eight of the people interviewed, four men and four women, had left work early through disability or health problems. All but one came from working-class backgrounds, some of them very poor. All had continued working up to and in some cases beyond the onset of their illnesses, until forced to retire through inability to continue in work. None had been unemployed when leaving the labour market, so they do not fall into the category of the older unemployed who 'vanish' from the figures through migration on to Incapacity Benefit. Most of them, however, continued to have active mental lives, taking part in adult education and leisure activities.

Despite these similarities, there is a gender difference in their current situations and income. The men with good retirement incomes were all happy and even Duncan, who also had a sick wife and lived in poverty, was quite happy. All had left work in their fifties. The women had on average left earlier than the men and had interrupted working lives that had adversely affected their pension entitlement. All were on poor or modest incomes and three were unhappy and dissatisfied with their lives. One, however, despite living on a low income with a long-term disabled husband and an unemployed son, was in very good spirits, mainly because she had discovered a talent for writing poetry through attending a creative writing class.

The people interviewed displayed characteristics that are not unique, but which are found to a greater degree in cities like Glasgow, such as lack of educational qualifications and basic skills, or job-specific skills that have been wiped out by deindustrialisation. Early negative experiences of the educational system had enduring effects and affected people's ability to adapt to rapid change and an increasingly competitive labour market, although as we have seen a number of those interviewed were proactive in pursuing education or skills. Wider evidence on these processes as they affect older people in the Scottish labour market are discussed by Hollywood et al (2003) and Novotný (2006).

Positive environmental factors

Despite these barriers, certain helping factors favourable to older workers were identified. The tight labour market, the current low birth rate and increased tendency for young people to stay longer in education mean that, all things being equal, the pool of labour is shrinking less than the demand for it. As long as the local economy does not seriously deteriorate, this potentially advantages older people in the labour market.

Older people with an employment history, even if interrupted, will often have positive attitudes to work, work discipline and the ability to work with others – as was seen in the interviews discussed above. These qualities are increasingly promoted officially with older workers being portrayed in Scotland as being reliable, loyal, having good customer skills and low rates of absenteeism (Brown, 2000). This makes older people increasingly attractive recruits to the retail and financial industries and jobs without great physical demands or extreme time pressures (Age Concern Policy Unit, 2004).

The anti-discrimination legislation introduced in 2006 will, despite its limitations, benefit older workers, as may the work of the Equality and Human Rights Commission (EHRC), discussed in Chapter Eleven. There is no doubt that, in addition, a radical cultural change in society's attitudes to age discrimination, particularly employers' attitudes, is required. The promotion of the business case for age diversity is being put forward by The Employers' Forum on Age, which states that:

> Ageism is deeply entrenched in society and the workplace. Valuing people of all ages within the workforce and regarding them all as a sustainable rather than a disposable resource is essential for our future prosperity. (www.efa. org.uk)

There are signs of a change in employer attitudes, in addition to the well-known case of B&Q, a large hardware chain that found it more profitable to include older workers on the shop floor. Firms such as the Nationwide Building Society and M&S have ended the mandatory retirement age. Halifax Bank of Scotland has a flexible approach to retirement: people can take career breaks and opt to work beyond retirement age.

Prospects for the future

We have already seen that some of the respondents in the sample were concerned about the jobs available in the labour market to them compared with life on benefits, or priorities for voluntary working or caring. Thus a range of options needs to be mapped out so that people can make genuine choices between full- and part-time work or self-employment, giving greater or less priority according to their choices of a life outside employment, traded against income possibilities. Work-life balance is an issue for everyone, of course, and not least those who may have more limited energy to pursue all possible life objectives at the same time. There needs to be recognition that other roles, such as grandparenting, or involvement in community life, are as valid as paid employment. There is also evidence that maintenance of social networks is a positive influence on health and longevity (IFS, 2006).

Many jobs in supermarkets – where increasing numbers of older employees are visible – are quite menial and may not be suitable for everyone, with limited prospects of career progression. There is a danger that older people may replace women in the eyes of some employers, seen as prepared to work for part-time 'pin-money' or to get out of the house for a while. This raises the question of whether some jobs taken in later life constitute a new start or merely exploitation. Work that is exploitative, menial, uninteresting or below the individual's capabilities may be tolerable only for a few hours per week.

Some who leave work for health reasons might well, with more support, have continued working longer, perhaps part time. Indeed, three women in the Glasgow SEQUAL research who reported health problems were still working, albeit part time or irregularly, and one man, who had taken early retirement after heart surgery, had retrained and was enjoying a second career as a teacher. Adult education had been important to all of them, either as a way of keeping mentally active and meeting other people or as a way of acquiring qualifications.

Legislation is important but insufficient. People who are unemployed because they are considered 'too old' as a consequence lose confidence and esteem by accepting that it is 'only right'. New Deals and other schemes do now increasingly seek to help older and disabled workers to remain in or access employment. Vocational guidance geared towards the needs of older people can assist in raising confidence, help people to recognise and develop their existing skills and advise them on further education and training useful for entering or returning to work. The 50+ age group is a priority group for Information, Advice and Guidance partnerships in England (Ford et al, 2003). Above all, with a degree of support from the state, the onus is placed on individuals to become employed. Very few responsibilities are placed on employers, who have a patchy record on training and support (Spence and Kelly, 2003).

This supply-side approach is inadequate, however, and a cultural shift is required from employers, which the 2006 age legislation may start to stimulate. In this respect vocational advice and guidance, therefore, is making positive links between employers and clients, for example, through organising work placements, work shadowing, informing local employers of likely candidates and collecting information about the local labour market and job opportunities as they arise. Local authorities and educational providers can also play an important role. For example, Glasgow has instituted a 50+ job rotation scheme, funded by the European Social Fund (ESF) and run by Glasgow City Council and the University of Strathclyde (50+ Challenge, 2004). This is aimed at small businesses in the private and voluntary sectors and the goals are to increase the skills and confidence of existing older workers, help retain them and give older unemployed workers and returners work experience. First, a training needs assessment and training plan are developed with the company, and mentoring is also provided. Next, a job rotation trainee, aged 50+ and previously unemployed or a labour market returner, undergoes relevant vocational training and a personal development programme. Finally, in return for releasing a minimum of four members of staff aged 50+ for training provided free by the scheme, the firm takes on the trainee for a minimum six-month contract of at least 25 hours at the going rate for the job. The job must be additional to the existing workforce. A £50 per week wage subsidy is also provided under the scheme.

Conclusion

Both the small-scale SEQUAL study and the wider evidence cited indicate that older people in Scotland and elsewhere in the UK encounter significant barriers to finding or keeping employment, or maintaining a decent standard of living after retirement. These include health and disability, inadequate or outmoded skills, combined with lack of confidence, age discrimination and poor access to help and support.

There is strong evidence that it is the most disadvantaged who face the greatest hurdles and who have the least chance of an adequate pension and further opportunities to pursue a fulfilling 'third age' in our present society.

Older people have much to contribute and disadvantaging them in the labour market is both a waste of valuable resources and unfair on those who wish to or need to continue working. Current pressures of demographic change and growing awareness of both the economic costs and social injustices associated with age discrimination, as well as the 2006 legislation, create an opportunity to challenge existing complacency. However, proposals to raise the pension age indicate that in some ways the world may get harder rather than easier for those most socially disadvantaged in old age. This will be tackled only if rights to a decent standard of life for all, both within and outside paid work, are acknowledged, to enable older people to make the employment choices that best suit them.

References

50+ Challenge (2004) *Glasgow 50+ job retention* (fiftyplus@strath. ac.uk).

Age Concern Policy Unit (2004) *The economy and older people*, London: Age Concern England.

Brown, R. (2000) *Getting old and grey?*, Glasgow and Inverness: Futureskills Scotland, Scottish Enterprise and Highlands and Islands Enterprise.

DWP (Department for Work and Pensions) (2005a) *Opportunity age: Volume two. A social portrait of ageing in the UK*, London: DWP.

DWP (2005b) *Older workers: Statistical information booklet, Spring*, London: DWP.

DWP (2006) *A new deal for welfare: Empowering people to work*, London: DWP.

Ford, G., Watkins, B., Bosley, S., Hawthorn, R., McGowan, B. and Grattan, P. (2003) *Challenging age: Information, advice and guidance for older age groups*, Sheffield: Department for Education and Skills.

Hanlon, P., Walsh, D. and Whyte, B. (2006) *Let Glasgow flourish: A comprehensive report on health and its determinants in Glasgow and West Central Scotland*, Glasgow: Glasgow Centre for Population Health.

HM Treasury (2006) *Prosperity for all in the global economy – World class skills: final report* (Leitch Report), London: The Stationery Office.

Hollywood, E., Brown, R., Danson, M. and McQuaid, R. (2003) *Older workers in the Scottish labour market: A new agenda*, Stirling: scotecon. net, University of Stirling.

IFS (Institute of Fiscal Studies) (2006) *Longitudinal study of ageing reveals health and wealth relationship*, London: IFS Press Release.

Irving, P., Steels, J. and Hall, N. (2005) *Factors affecting the labour market participation of older workers: Qualitative research*, DWP Research Report No 281, London: Department for Work and Pensions.

Lewis, D. and Sargeant, M. (2007) *Essentials of employment law* (9th edn), London: Chartered Institute of Personnel and Development.

Loretto, W., Vickerstaff, S. and White, P. (2006) *Older workers and options for flexible work*, Working Paper Series No 31, Manchester: Equal Opportunities Commission.

McKay, S. and Middleton, S. (1998) *Characteristics of older workers: Secondary analysis of the family and working lives survey*, Report No RR45, London: Department for Education and Employment.

Novotný, V. (2006) *Older people and employment in Scotland*, Strathclyde: Centre for Lifelong Learning, University of Strathclyde.

O'Neill, R. (2006) 'Not dead yet', *Hazards Magazine*, no 96, October/December (www.hazards.org/olderworkers/index.htm).

Pensions Commission (2007) *A new pension settlement for the twenty-first century: The second report of the Pensions Commission*, London: The Stationery Office.

Plant, P. (2005) 'Gerento guidance? Third age guidance', *Newsletter of the International Association for Education and Vocational Guidance*, no 51, February.

Ray, S., Sharp, E. and Abrams, D. (2006) *Ageism: A benchmark of public attitudes in Britain*, London: Age Concern England.

Scottish Executive (2003) *Inequalities in health: Report of the Measuring Inequalities in Health Working Group*, Edinburgh: Scottish Executive.

Spence, J. and Kelly, A. (2003) *Tremplin: The mismatch of skills on the labour market – An analysis and solutions provided by training*, Luxembourg: Prism Research and Consulting SARL.

The Scottish Government (2006) *Annual population survey in Scotland 2005*, Part 9 (www.scotland.gov.uk/Publications/2006/06/28140032/9).

Vickerstaff, S. (2006) 'Entering the retirement zone: how much choice do individuals have?', *Social Policy and Society*, vol 5, no 4, pp 507-17.

NINE

Refugees and the labour market: refugee sector practice in the 'employability' paradigm

Azar Sheibani

Introduction: key issues

This chapter examines the refugee sector's role in facilitating refugee entry into the labour market in the UK and the barriers faced by refugees in an environment dominated by tightening borders, tough legislation and policies, the current 'employability' model, employers' prejudice and discrimination and general hostility towards refugees and asylum seekers. The aim is to examine how practice at agency level could be influenced by and can influence policy and how a global understanding of refugee issues can affect the way refugees are treated at local level. This is of particular significance in a European context since the strength of the voluntary and community sector in the UK is unparalleled in Europe.

The analysis relies on the voices of refugees, drawing on the findings of the SEQUAL research carried out by London Metropolitan University and the work of the Refugee Assessment and Guidance Unit (RAGU) as one of the chief agencies in London responsible for the development and delivery of a range of services to refugees and asylum seekers in the fields of education, training and employment.

The research was carried out in a rapidly changing environment for refugees, following the publication in 2005 of two major policies by the Home Office and the Department for Work and Pensions, which subsequently led to many changes. In order to locate the chapter in a wider context it is essential to have a brief look at the refugee situation at the UK and global level. Although the chapter focuses on London it has a national relevance. It relies on the voices of refugees, the agencies that support them and employers. Refugees' employment prospects are examined in the light of broader government policies and the limitations they impose.

Setting the scene: refugees, government policies and the labour market

The Office of United Nations High Commissioner for Refugees (UNHCR) published its most recent report on refugees in April 2006. The number of refugees fell 12% in 2005 to 8.4 million (UNHCR, 2006). The fall in Europe is mainly due to tightening borders and the 'deterrence' policies on asylum. Since September 2001, the European states have become more concerned with international terrorism and security issues and have become increasingly restrictive towards asylum seekers and refugees.

It is impossible to separate forced international migration from the accelerated rate of globalisation. The problem arises when transnational corporations and governments welcome the free movement of 'capital' while wanting to control the movements of 'labour' and people in general. In the EU states the response has been to tighten the borders and toughen up legislation to control entry. Since 1980 in the UK alone, there have been 14 pieces of legislation or new rules relating to refugees and asylum seekers, signifying the importance that the state now assigns to border controls, the numbers who enter, the profile of those who enter and integration and citizenship issues (Schuster, 2003).

In the UK, there are no accurate and reliable statistics on the number of refugees. The Home Office records indicate that between 2001 and 2005 a total of 144,000 refugees were granted leave to remain in the UK. In 2004, Jobcentre Plus introduced a voluntary marker to identify refugee claimants and 70,000 records have been collected. Nearly half of all refugees reside in London compared with the other main areas of settlement: West Midlands (10%), Yorkshire and Humberside (8%), North West (8%) and Scotland and Wales (5%) (Jobcentre Plus, 2005). Conservative official estimates record refugee unemployment at six times the national average and for some refugee communities the rate is much higher (DWP, 2005). Research by the Department for Work and Pensions in 2003 concluded that only 29% of refugees were working, compared with 60% of the minority ethnic population and 94% of the White settled population (DWP, 2003).

The emphasis on controlling borders and deterring asylum seekers is at odds with policies of 'inclusion' and 'integration' for those who are granted asylum. Deterrence policies would not be effective if refugees were treated well. In 2005/06, a total of 25,155 people applied for asylum, which was 21% lower than in 2004/05 (Home Office, 2006). Hostility towards refugees has become pervasive, with popular misconceptions about refugees being reinforced by politicians, who demand tough action against 'bogus asylum seekers and economic migrants':

> Deterrence and hostility are largely a result of the Immigration and Asylum Act 1999, the Nationality, Immigration and Asylum Act 2002 and the Asylum and Immigration (Treatment of Claimants) Act 2004. (Addis and Morrow, 2005, p 285)

It was not until 2005 that the government seriously addressed 'integration' with the publication of two major policy papers. In March 2005, the Home Office published its national strategy for refugee integration, *Integration matters*, and, in the same year, the Department for Work and Pensions published their refugee employment strategy, *Working to rebuild lives*. The following examples illustrate how the recent rulings by the Home Office are in conflict with the above strategies.

In August 2005, the Home Office removed the right of refugees to indefinite leave to remain on the granting of 'refugee status' and limited the initial 'leave to remain' to five years after which there would be a review. This will actively discourage employers from considering refugees for employment as their residential status is not certain and subject to review. The 'five-year' ruling therefore undermines the Home Office's strategy paper on 'integration' of refugees and ways of engaging them. In the same year the Home Office decided that as soon as refugees got citizenship, they could no longer be entitled to the support programmes specifically designed for refugees. The citizenship paper does not change the refugees' status for employers, professional bodies and society and cannot eliminate discrimination and racism. It is ironic that 'citizenship' in this instance reduces refugees' chances of acquiring the knowledge, skills and experience to engage as citizens and delays their journey towards citizenship.

Refugees in London and their employment prospects

The London Metropolitan University SEQUAL research sought the experiences and views of refugees, the refugee agencies and employers in order to compare and contrast the narratives of each group and to construct a holistic picture.

We were unable, in the project, to target asylum seekers who did not have permission to work. 'Asylum seekers' are those who have applied for asylum and are awaiting the Home Office decision. They are unable to take employment unless they have been granted permission to work.

They can apply for permission to work if they have been waiting for more than 12 months for their initial decision on their asylum claim from the Home Office. Only the main applicants for asylum can apply for permission to work and this means that if the main applicant is the husband, his wife will not have a right to apply for permission to work. Asylum seekers are not eligible for government training schemes even if they have permission to work. Asylum seekers will only be entitled to free ESOL (English for Speakers of Other Languages) classes six months after their claim for asylum.

The research focused on London because of its unique position in accommodating refugees. The numbers of refugees and asylum seekers in London are estimated at between 350,000 and 420,000, or about 1 in 20 of the city's resident population. This is a proportion around 30 times greater than the UK average. The Greater London Authority (GLA) claims that the skill levels of asylum seekers are above the host society's average (GLA, 2001).

Refugees are not a homogeneous group but the following are some of the main barriers that affect refugees by varying degrees:

- conflicting government policies
- employers' prejudice and racism
- institutional barriers such as professional bodies' lengthy and expensive requalification requirements
- the media's negative portrayal of refugees and asylum seekers
- refugees' absence from 'race' relations legislation
- lack of recognition of refugees' previous qualifications and experience
- lack of work experience and references in the UK
- the 'poverty trap' for most refugee families where only one spouse is likely to work and the family income is likely to be less than the state benefits
- lack of access to appropriate and specialist information, advice and guidance services for refugees
- inadequate knowledge and skills of mainstream agencies to deal with refugees
- lack of appropriate and adequate English language provision
- refugees' inadequate language and communication skills
- lack of knowledge and awareness of UK work culture
- lack of adequate childcare and support provision for refugee women
- employment barriers for some refugee women with children and family responsibilities.

An important finding of this research was the decisive role of refugees and their determination to overcome the barriers and to secure jobs. The overwhelming evidence from our 11 years' experience of working in this field supports the findings of the research.

Refugees' voices

Refugees had well-formed views about employers. They generally felt that employers were reluctant to employ refugees and stated various reasons for employers' reluctance, such as cultural fit, language or accent and citizenship (all names that follow have been anonymised):

> 'I am thinking maybe if I change my name at least they can shortlist me and see my work [so they're] not just thinking about my name as a foreign person.' (Nazgol, from Iran)

Our research endorsed other research findings (Sargeant et al, 1999; Bloch, 2002, 2004) that refugees' qualifications and experience are largely undervalued or not recognised at all by employers, professional bodies, NARIC (National Recognition and Information Centre) and universities:

> 'If you are not strong enough you can get mad, you can get – because totally your life changes, you have to start from the beginning and to prove for the people you are a person with qualifications and experiences.' (Fozia, a researcher from Sudan)

> 'When you have been educated at a higher level you feel frustrated because you know when you talk about your skills, everybody laughs at you ... it's because you didn't do it here, it's not a skill. That is horrible.' (Nia, a teacher from Central Africa)

Asking for UK work experience from a refugee was again an easy way of rejecting them:

> 'I've attended I think quite a lot of interviews where they've always asked me this question that I find very, very ah difficult to understand ... because I say to you I've just arrived and you are saying for this job I need somebody

who has worked here for seven years.' (Claude, from Cameroon)

Ignoring and casting doubt on overseas qualifications and experience is a safe strategy, which can be used by employers to reject refugees, as these areas are not covered by any legislation. The interviews with employers revealed that they largely limit the application of their 'equality and diversity' agenda to the settled minority ethnic groups and for various reasons do not consider refugees as those who should be covered by these policies.

The refugees who were interviewed were of the view that employers did not consider them as culturally fit for the organisation:

'You fill in an application form, you give them all the necessary information and during the interview, because they discover you are a refugee they start asking you questions.' (Claude, from Cameroon)

Interviews with employers confirmed this prejudice as they suggested that refugees could be employed only if they could integrate into the workplace seamlessly:

'It's also the ability to actually seamlessly integrate with a new group of workers, and that is hard for a lot of people, and I suspect it's even harder for someone who comes from a culturally different background.' (Director of a recruitment agency)

Non-European, non-White cultures were often regarded as incompatible with the prevailing western culture. This 'cultural compatibility' can work as a shield to hide prejudice and racism.

All respondents believed that the media had contributed to the negative portrayal of refugees and asylum seekers and had made the employers and the wider society more suspicious of them. Mirroring the tougher government policies on asylum seekers and refugees, the media representations of refugees emphasise their potential threat as 'terrorists' and 'benefit scroungers'. The respondents who identified themselves as Muslims experienced this suspicious attitude more acutely and felt that their religion and Islamic names deterred employers from considering them for employment. Compared with settled Muslim communities, they had the added disadvantage of not knowing about their rights and the legislation that could protect them.

The situation for the refugees who do not identify themselves as religious but who have come from Islamic countries is also difficult but in a different way. They have fled repressive Islamic regimes and extremist groups and their refugee status is a testimony to the persecution they experienced but, as refugees coming from Islamic countries, they find themselves labelled as Muslim terrorists in the receiving country, which is a bitter irony.

The refugee respondents were desperate to get a voluntary position to prove their skills and the picture was far from what the media tried to impose:

> 'I did even offer them; I don't want any salary please. I don't want anything ... I was prepared to work for six months, seven days a week until I pick up the experience.' (Alem, a business graduate from Ethiopia)

A fundamental issue, which is usually neglected, is the hierarchical nature of support for refugees. The needs of refugee professionals receive more attention and coverage and the main argument presented is that many of them are highly qualified and can contribute to the host society, so their skills should not be neglected. While this might be a useful argument in some instances, their potential or immediate contribution should not be the basis for supporting refugees. They should be supported because they are refugees, not because they are highly educated and are able to make an economic contribution. This approach introduces a complex hierarchical order among refugees based on their level of education, class and social status.

How does the dominant 'employability' model affect refugees?

One of the key findings of this research was that most strategies and practices focus on refugees themselves. This 'deficit' model puts the onus for achieving employability on individual refugees and suggests that if the shortcomings of individuals could be addressed, they could be brought to the right level in order to compete fairly in the labour market. This mirrors the current 'employability' model advocated by New Labour and the emphasis on supply-side and micro-level policy interventions through welfare-to-work policies. Peck and Theodore (2000) argue that, in this model, the supply side of the labour market is considered to be both the cause of and the solution to unemployment. The emphasis is on the motivation and flexibility of unemployed people while neglecting the state's responsibility to create jobs (Peck and Theodore, 2000). This is evident in the current targeting of 'worklessness' and the rhetoric around it.

To overcome the numerous barriers they face, refugees resort to various strategies, which rely heavily on their individual resources and adaptability. They go for lower-level jobs and adjust their CVs to hide their higher level of education. The following is one of the numerous examples that we witness in our daily work with refugees:

> 'I applied to different organisations and sent them my CV. I had different interviews ... most of them contacted me and said "you are over-skilled and over-qualified". That was a problem so I changed my CV and I just reduced the qualifications that I had and the years of experience and everything ... and then got more interviews.' (Farrokh, from Iran)

The 'deficit' model has been internalised by refugees and they take it on themselves to 'fit' within the workplace and so constantly lower their expectations.

Employers also adhere to this dominant model. They view refugees as in need of remedial actions and extra resources and refer to the lack of additional resources to accommodate refugees.

Most refugee respondents were critical of job centres' attitude and practices. They reported that the job centres pressurised them to accept any type of job. They felt that their 'country of origin', 'accent' and probable 'lack of fluency in the English language' meant that advisers did not value their qualifications and work experience from their home countries. This claim is supported by refugee agencies. They were of the view that job centre advisers predominantly undervalued refugees' qualifications and experience:

> 'There is a problem with the job centre ... they're often encouraged to do any type of job which may be way beneath their education, their intellectual ability so it's like doctors ending up as cleaners and warehouse people ... they do seem to be very driven by government targets to getting people into work.' (Respondent from a refugee sector organisation)

Another barrier that all groups of respondents identified was ambiguity about refugees' legal status. Some employers were genuinely worried and were not clear about refugees' immigration status, as expressed by one of our respondents:

> 'I can't say that I know all the different groups what their entitlements are. My understanding is that refugees are not entitled to undertake paid employment.' (Employer)

Refugees' 'refuge'

Another key finding from the research was the unique and irreplaceable contribution of the refugee sector organisations in facilitating refugees' entry into the labour market and their settlement and integration in the UK. This is unique in Europe partly because of the strength of the voluntary sector in the UK and partly because, up to very recently, the state did not have any strategy on reception and resettlement of refugees and the vacuum was filled by refugee community organisations and refugee agencies.

In the UK, the refugee sector plays a pivotal role at all stages of refugee settlement. The existence of more than 300 refugee support agencies in London alone shows the strength of the sector and the resilience of refugees themselves. They have transformed both their own lives and their communities and have put their experience and skills to use. The refugee sector organisations are often the only spaces where refugees feel that they are treated with the dignity that they deserve and where their experience of being a refugee is understood and respected. The reality is that in the receiving country, refugees find themselves escaping once more – this time from the harsh and humiliating environment that they experience on a daily basis – to the refugee support agencies. The refugee respondents in our research testified that the refugee sector organisations were the only agencies that supported refugees' access to the labour market at a level commensurate with their previous education and experience.

The agencies that were interviewed had introduced innovative initiatives and interventions to support refugees including refugee-centred approaches, special accelerated training programmes to refresh skills, placement programmes and holistic approaches targeting refugees, employers and policy makers simultaneously:

> '[It is] very intensive so it involves advice and guidance, it involves training, it involves liaison with employers and it involves you know, lobbying and raising awareness on

a much broader scale than just on an individual level.'
(Refugee agency respondent)

Work placement schemes are among the promising practices in this sector. A successful model includes working with refugees and employers to broker an appropriate placement, intensive training to familiarise refugees with the work environment, awareness raising among employers, providing support to refugees and employers during the placement and writing good practice guidelines for organisations offering placements.

The research demonstrated that while the refugee sector worked within the 'employability' paradigm and the tight parameters set by the government and funders, at the micro-level they managed to introduce initiatives enabling refugees to regain their lost confidence in order to overcome unfavourable policies and prejudice, discrimination and racism.

The refugee sector makes an irreplaceable contribution but its influence remains marginal as agencies are governed and limited by government policies and funders. For example, they experience a real dilemma when they find themselves rejecting refugees with 'citizenship' papers in circumstances where they are aware of the need but are not allowed to offer their service to naturalised refugees. Their everyday work is fraught with continual battles with job centres and other mainstream agencies to negotiate solutions out of constant deadlocks. Those who fund the employment support initiatives expect job outcomes at the end of relatively short periods of intervention. This leaves refugee agencies in the undesirable position of either losing part of the funding or compromising their client-centred approach and surrendering to 'underemployment'.

The refugee sector representatives commented that there was very little government acknowledgement of the refugee sector's role in service delivery to refugees and that they were often given marginal roles. Since 2005 this has started to change, as there are various attempts at national and regional level to set up partnerships with the refugee sector and to give more weight to their contribution. The Department for Work and Pensions' 'refugee employment strategy' sets to involve the voluntary sector as partners in their delivery programmes. Several pilots have started in some regions including London but it is too early to determine whether they could be mainstreamed.

The refugee sector organisations are making inroads to influence employers but the dominant culture drives them to rely on business cases rather than a 'rights-based' approach, which they cannot easily mobilise in the absence of strong policy back-up.

Nearly all studies on refugees and human rights have concentrated on 'asylum' rights of residence of individuals, and the 'human rights' approach is not extended to conditions of integration, including employment. Hathaway (2005) has referred to six international instruments regarding refugees' wage-earning rights but these have never been utilised to influence policies regarding refugees' socio-economic rights. In the same vein, Craven argues:

> There is no international guarantee of a right actually to secure work, only freely to seek work. (Craven, 1995, p 203)

'Equality and diversity' and 'language' as legitimised tools of discrimination

A significant finding of the SEQUAL research is that refugees are not mentioned and are often formally excluded in major policies and legislation on 'equality and diversity'. Thus, the 1976 Race Relations Act and the 2000 Race Relations (Amendment) Act, in outlawing discrimination, make exceptions of the state's immigration and nationality functions, Section 19D legally enshrining the state's right to discriminate on grounds of nationality, or ethnic or national origins. Refugees are not defined as a racial group for the purposes of 'race relations' legislation, and this has not been remedied by the creation of the Equality and Human Rights Commission (EHRC) and nor will it be changed by the forthcoming Single Equality Act (Refugee Council, 2004, pp 4, 5). In 2001, a Council of Europe survey found that racism against asylum seekers and refugees was 'particularly acute' in Britain, and fuelled by 'xenophobic and intolerant' media coverage and politicians' speeches. The Council criticised Britain's 'increasingly restrictive asylum and immigration laws' (Black, 2001).

The special role that language plays is a further important finding of this research and our centre's work with refugees. In this context, 'language' is seen as a sociopolitical phenomenon (Chomsky, 1975), which is much broader than a set of grammatical expressions and ways of speaking a language. For employers and mainstream agencies, 'language' encompasses country of origin, class, status, ethnicity and culture. In the absence of any legislative coverage, it can be used to sanitise and legitimise prejudice against refugees and to define them as 'those who don't know our way of life'. In our centre, the advisers see refugees on a daily basis. A considerable number of them state that they find 'language' and 'communication skills' to be barriers but believe that employers exaggerate them and use them indiscriminately even against those with good language skills or whose first language is English. Language is frequently used as a subjective marker of 'otherness' to rule out a refugee candidate rather than an objective measurement of their ability to work in the given field and to communicate effectively in the workplace. In the case of refugees whose first language is English, 'language' is used to disguise the prejudice against their 'country of origin'.

Other studies have identified 'language' as a key barrier to employment of refugees (for example, Sargeant et al, 1999; Bloch, 2004). The Refugee Skills Net found that 48% of refugees who spoke fluent English were still unemployed (London Research Centre, 1999).

The relationship between 'employment' and 'integration'

The definition of integration for refugees varies and there is a considerable gap between written policies and practices. The Home Office's expectation of integration is different from refugees' and refugee communities' expectations. This has had a significant impact on refugees' settlement in the UK. The differing and sometimes conflicting views of integration agree that employment is one step towards integration but they differ significantly on how employment is achieved and what autonomy the refugees have in choosing their job.

Our research demonstrated that when refugees secured jobs they were often underemployed beneath the level of their skills or qualifications. This was either self-imposed (as an individual strategy to fight poverty and stigma) or imposed by external factors. Underemployment is neither 'emancipatory' nor 'empowering'. Labour market conditions and the current political climate reinforce this model. The underemployed refugees feel 'undervalued' and 'humiliated' and as long as this is the case, they can never feel 'integrated'.

The EU's overemphasis on the role of paid employment as the determining factor in integration leads in most cases to eurocentric assimilatory practices. In this paradigm, integration is measured through attainment of a job and political, civic and cultural rights are essentially ignored. However, Levitas argues:

The term 'work' is restricted to market-based activity and excludes much socially necessary labour. (Levitas, 2001, p 450)

For a refugee, employment might not be seen as a step towards genuine integration, especially if it is 'underemployment'. Many refugees remain unemployed but their contribution in economic, civic, social, cultural and political terms is invaluable to their communities in exile:

It has to be recognised that neither the right to an income, nor full citizenship, nor everyone's sense of identity and self-fulfilment can any longer be centred on and depend on occupying a job. And society has to be changed to take account of this. (Gorz, 1999, p 54)

In the case of refugees and their communities, the above statement is apt. The research reinforced the fact that while for some refugees employment is an important step en route to integration, others embraced a broader conception of social involvement and citizenship.

Conclusion: linking 'local' practices to 'global' perspectives

Our research sought to build a more accurate picture of 'refugee employment' through refugees' own interpretations, refugee sector agencies' views and experiences, and employers' views and practices. This chapter has also relied on 11 years' collective experience of RAGU in working with refugees, refugee agencies, major partnerships, employers, funders and government departments to facilitate refugees' satisfactory entry into higher education and the labour market.

Refugee support agencies have a pivotal role in facilitating refugees' entry into the labour market but the impact is mainly felt at micro levels. These initiatives sometimes extend beyond the boundaries of the 'employability' paradigm and offer innovative ideas to make refugees' journey towards employment more humane, without undermining their previous learning or experience. However, their impact is limited by restrictive government policies.

Government departments partly fund the employment support services for refugees, and the Home Office's integration policy promises increased support for the refugee sector, including a refugee integration website, improving consultation with refugee community organisations, SUNRISE (Strategic Upgrade of Natural Refugee Integration Services) and encouraging positive images of refugees (Home Office, 2005). However, their overarching policy of deterrence undermines integration and employment policies, which seriously dents their effectiveness.

The chapter has also argued that the exclusion of refugees from major 'equality and diversity' policies and legislation in the UK has seriously curtailed their access and rights to decent employment. Refugees' exclusion from 'race' relations legislation has meant that employers can conceal the discriminatory and prejudicial practices under pretexts such as 'lack of fluency in English language', 'ambiguous immigration status', 'cultural mismatch' and 'lack of resource to support refugees in the workplace'.

This chapter demonstrates that the promising practices exist at 'local' level despite restrictive and conflicting policies and an often hostile environment in the wider society. The dominant 'employability' model holds the unemployed refugees responsible for their shortcomings and asks them to 'recycle' themselves in order to become 'fit' and respond to the shortages of the receiving society. The current approach to promoting refugee employment predominantly relies on 'business case' logic: emphasising refugees' skills and contribution towards the receiving society and the benefits they might yield. This model might secure employment for some refugees but will not promote full and fair integration.

A shift from a 'deficit' to a 'rights-based' model is needed to escape the current deadlock. The piecemeal approaches within a 'deficit' model and conflicting policies will offer very little to enable refugees to 'rebuild' their lives with full access to social, civic, cultural and economic rights. Promising practices cannot be mainstreamed if they are not supported by legislation, government policies and major shifts in the dominant paradigm of seeing refugees as 'in permanent debt' to the receiving society. There is a need to inject a global perspective into all levels of intervention from state policy to local initiatives and advocacy practices in order to promote refugees' employability. Every opportunity should be used to link the everyday dilemmas of refugees to global issues and forced migration and to broaden the horizons of those who are inclined to see refugees as a 'burden'.

References

Addis, M. and Morrow, P. (2005) *Your rights: The Liberty guide to human rights* (8th edn), London: Pluto Press.

Black, I. (2001) 'UK "most racist" in Europe on refugees', *The Guardian*, 3 April.

Bloch, A. (2002) *Refugees' opportunities and barriers in employment and training*, Research Report 179, Leeds: Department for Work and Pensions.

Bloch, A. (2004) *Making it work: Refugee employment in the UK*, London: Institute for Public Policy Research.

Chomsky, N. (1975) *The logical structure of linguistic theory*, New York, NY: Penguin.

Craven, M. (1995) *The International Covenant on Economic, Social and Cultural Rights: A perspective on its development*, Oxford: Clarendon Press.

DWP (Department for Work and Pensions) (2003) *Working to rebuild lives: A preliminary report towards a refugee employment strategy*, London: DWP.

DWP (2005) *Working to rebuild lives: A refugee employment strategy*, London: DWP.

GLA (Greater London Authority) (2001) *Refugees and asylum seekers in London: A GLA perspective, Draft report for consultation*, London: GLA Policy Support Unit.

Gorz, A. (1999) *Reclaiming work: Beyond the wage-based society*, Cambridge: Polity Press.

Hathaway, J.C. (2005) *The rights of refugees under international law*, New York, NY: Cambridge University Press.

Home Office (2005) *Integration matters: A national strategy for refugee integration*, London: IND Corporate Communications.

Home Office (2006) 'Immigration and Nationality Directorate quarterly asylum statistics' (www.homeoffice.gov.uk/rds/immigration1.html).

Jobcentre Plus (2005) *Working together to help rebuild lives: A framework for partnership working to help refugees fulfil their potential*, London: Jobcentre Plus.

Levitas, R. (2001) 'Against work: a utopian incursion into social policy', *Critical Social Policy*, vol 21, no 4, pp 449-65.

London Research Centre (1999) *The employment and training of skilled and qualified refugees*, London: Refugees Skills Net.

Peck, J. and Theodore, N. (2000) 'Beyond employability', *Cambridge Journal of Economics*, vol 24, no 6, pp 729-49.

Refugee Council (2004) *The Refugee Council's response to the government's White Paper: 'Fairness for all: A new Commission for Equality and Human Rights'*, London: Refugee Council.

Sargeant, G., Damachi, D. and Long, D. (1999) *'Turning refugees into employees': Do study grants help refugees find jobs?*, London: The Nuffield Foundation.

Schuster, L. (2003) *The use and abuse of political asylum in Britain and Germany*, London: Frank Cass Publishers.

UNHCR (Office of the United Nations High Commissioner for Refugees) (2006) *The state of the world's refugees: Human displacement in the new millennium*, Oxford: Oxford University Press.

Part Two
Implications for wider policies

Origins and effects of New Labour's workfare state: modernisation or variations on old themes?

Mick Carpenter with Stuart Speeden

Introduction: realising the promise of promising practices

This chapter and Chapter Eleven move on from local case studies and specific forms of disadvantage to a more general analysis, drawing on the 'lessons' of the case studies and wider available evidence. This chapter is primarily concerned with a review and critical assessment of economic and social policies towards the workfare state up to and since 1997 under New Labour. Chapter Eleven then develops a discussion of policy alternatives beyond it, connecting them to emerging campaigns to combat forms of discrimination and to promote equalities and human rights.

Disputing first the idea that New Labour's welfare policy is entirely a 'modernising' project, this chapter locates recent reforms within an enduring British liberal tradition of economic and social policy, arguing that this remains a key weakness on both economic and social justice grounds. It then outlines the broader policy context in which the employment-focused community-based initiatives (CBIs) featured in the earlier chapters expanded under New Labour after 1997. It acknowledges the progress made from the point of view of economically disadvantaged and discriminated-against communities but also identifies a plateau in terms of policy impact on unemployment and 'worklessness' from the Labour government's third term after 2005. The government's response has been to rely on supply-side approaches, such as skills training and the intensification of compulsion and sanctions against unemployed and workless people, exemplified by the 2007 Welfare Reform Act and the Freud report (2007). This reliance on the agency of individuals and communities is shown to be deficient as an explanation of 'welfare dependency' and/or reluctance to enter the labour market and is therefore a poor starting point for labour market policy. A socially informed structure–agency explanation is developed that gives scope to local initiatives and individual action while recognising the need to address the wider political economy and structural inequalities.

Continuity and change before the contemporary workfare state

The enduring liberal inheritance

New Labour has been critical of the Conservative governments from 1979 to 1997 for allowing unemployment to rise and for failing to provide effective supply-side measures, and has also distanced itself from the previous social democratic era. There is a need to sort myth from reality:

> From the 1940s to the 1970s government sought to address social and economic problems through intervention and state planning. Social democrats in Britain and the US who held a liberal view of the 'permissive society' divorced fairness from personal responsibility. They believed that the state had an unconditional obligation to provide welfare and security. The logic was that the individual owed nothing in return. (Blair, 2002)

This mythology has served to underpin the government's belief that rights are not 'inalienable', which is how they are often seen within the human rights approach discussed in more detail in Chapter Eleven next. Rather, they are seen in terms of a set of scales in which rights need to balance responsibilities. Once pictured in this way, the removal of rights can be defined not only as necessary but also as a benign process. This approach was restated by John Hutton, the Minister for Work and Pensions, in commending the recommendations of the Freud (2007) report on welfare reform discussed later in this chapter, aimed at 'rebalancing rights and responsibilities in the welfare system'.

Thus, while there has been change, there has also been continuity, in both economic and social policy, in which Thatcher and Blair have drawn on an enduring liberal tradition upholding the work ethic, which was enshrined in the 1942 Beveridge Report:

> The correlative of the State's undertaking to ensure adequate benefit for unavoidable interruption of earnings, however long, is enforcement of the citizen's obligation to seek and accept all reasonable opportunities of work. (Beveridge, 1942, para 130)

There was undoubtedly a partial turn away from laissez-faire political economy and Poor Law welfare policy from the early 20th century as part of a shift to 'managed capitalism', in which the state up to the 1970s had the prime responsibility to ensure 'full' employment. There has certainly been a turn away from demand-side management since 1979, the essential features of which have been maintained by New Labour after 1997.

Our exploration of these issues is mindful of three contrasting approaches. First, materialist or structuralist accounts explain changing policies as responses to the 'needs' of a changing capitalist economy, shaped from above by the changing interests of dominant classes, but which can be excessively deterministic. Second, idealist approaches by contrast see policy as arising from ideology or discourse, influential 'ideologies of welfare', as sometimes can be seen as championed by key individuals such as Keynes or Beveridge (for example, George and Wilding, 1985), with change occurring through ideological contestation. Third, both these processes may be seen as mediated by collective political mobilisation by classes and other social groups from below, of which Esping-Andersen's (1990) account of the resulting emergence of different welfare capitalisms is the most renowned. Our view is that a critical realist approach, as briefly outlined in Chapter One, can synthesise all three by analysing the interplay between material pressures, discourse and individual and collective agency.

Thus, within a strong materialist framework, Jessop (1994) portrays the shift towards a full employment society, and then the move away from it, as both primarily necessitated by wider capitalist economic imperatives. Intervention is seen as primarily arising from capital's needs to ensure mass consumption of standardised industrial products, as well as the social integration of working classes, leading to the creation of the Keynesian welfare state. We have already shown that there were rather 'weak' moves in this direction in the UK, influenced by enduring liberal traditions. Thus, ideology and political process were significant, as shown by the discursive or 'post-structuralist' account of the origins of interventionism developed by Walters (2000), who does to some extent link these to class mobilisation. He argues that the 'concept' or idea of unemployment was politically constructed from above through elite concern with the political consequences of 'decent' working-class men sinking into the 'residuum' or underclass through cyclical unemployment and chronic casualisation; and from below by the labour movement's articulation of a man's (and sometimes a woman's) 'right to work'. However, Walters does not give sufficient weight to the fact that the rising labour and socialist movement forced the issue onto the agenda by its collective industrial and political muscle. Unemployment was not just a 'concept' or discourse but an adverse 'reality' affecting the daily lives of ordinary people that they were mobilising to change. The combination of those material, ideological and political influences started to yield results through interventions by the Liberal government of 1906-14, reflected in shifts towards the 'public organisation of the labour market'. The more liberal, rather than full-blooded, statist approaches proposed by socialists such as the Webbs, became institutionally embedded with enduring effects (Walters, 2000, chapter 2). While the strength of these liberal traditions derived partly from ideology, their roots lay in the fact that British capitalism had emerged from below, which led to a negative view of the state, a growing dominance of commercial and financial interests and a strengthening of Poor Law principles in social policy. Despite relative economic decline, and challenges to imperialist hegemony, it was difficult to radically shift from the established pathway (Gamble, 1994). The requirements of state organisation for 'total war' on two occasions, and the associated strengthened power of labour, led to the most significant inroads into this tradition.

In terms of economic and social policy, the Edwardian era did see some shifts towards interventionism, with practical measures including the establishment of Trade Boards in 1909 to regulate wages and conditions in sweated trades, and labour exchanges intended to make the labour market work more efficiently and to eliminate the need for workers to 'hawk' themselves from one employer to another. Their purpose, as Beveridge put it in 1909, was 'making the finding of work easy instead of merely making relief hard' (cited by Price, 2000, p 4). The development of Unemployment Insurance in selected male trades in 1911, extended to most other trades by 1920, represented a significant shift away from the deterrent Poor Law and temporary 'Unemployment Relief'. To prevent malingering, and subsequent 'demoralisation', or what today would be called 'welfare dependency' – enduring British policy concerns – in contrast to other countries, labour exchanges were given the responsibility of administering and paying benefits. Strict eligibility rules disqualified workers from benefit for six weeks if they had been sacked for misconduct or left work voluntarily, a disqualification extended by the Conservatives to 26 weeks much later, in 1988 (Price, 2000, p 23).

From the outset, then, and thereafter, the British system as Price (2000, p 3) argues, has sought to reconcile three contradictory objectives of benefit control, devolved adaptation to local labour market conditions and sensitive attention to the welfare needs of unemployed people. At various times, the emphasis has swung from one to another, and since 1997 New Labour has sought to produce innovative ways of prioritising all three. During the interwar years, when the insurance system came under pressure from mass unemployment, the benefit control features came to the fore, through strict means testing and the setting of 'genuinely seeking work' conditions, which were relaxed from the 1940s to the 1970s. In the 1980s, there was a reversion to earlier approaches and 'actively seeking work' provisions became enshrined in the landmark Jobseeker's Allowance reform of 1996, the foundation on which New Labour welfare-to-work policies have been built.

In the 1940s, there was undoubtedly a shift to interventionism in the wake of total war, and then with the election of the Labour government in 1945, but the employment policy system that emerged by stages was still distinctly more liberal than socialist. While the 1944 employment policy White Paper committed governments to making full employment their first economic priority, the means chosen was a limited, or what Tomlinson (1994, p 269) calls a 'hydraulic' Keynesianism based on short-term economic management methods, producing 'stop-go' cycles that finally ran aground in the 1970s. This contrasted with some other European countries. Sweden, in particular, developed more extensive Keynesian intervention and more extensive social security and, stronger corporatist planning between the state, unions and employers, alongside active labour market policies that made generous unemployment benefits conditional on retraining and transfer to productive sectors (Calmfors et al, 2001). In contrast to Britain's patriarchal emphasis on full male employment, Sweden also pioneered a 'dual breadwinner' model, backed up by provision of childcare (Lewis, 1992). In Britain, trade unions clung to voluntary collective bargaining and governments to economic liberalism. Employers preferred to keep a distance from government, pursuing short-run profits rather than long-term investment, which was arguably a major influence on relative economic decline (Hutton, 1995).

The turn away from limited interventionism

In 1990, Esping-Andersen categorised the British welfare state as closer to the US 'liberal' model in terms of limited 'decommodification', that is, the extent to which working people could access a living income outside the labour market, compared to the more 'socialist' Scandinavian countries. We have already analysed the deep roots of this welfare regime. In specific terms, however, it was due to the 1945-51 Labour government's acceptance of Beveridge's flat-rate benefits, set low to reinforce work incentives. The (male, able-bodied) right to work was achieved primarily by the general strength of the postwar economy, underwritten more by Keynesianism at the international level than by the feeble national version.

Conservative governments, in shifting to a more restrictive approach after 1979, were arguably able to do so because of the weakly embedded nature of British Keynesianism, the final erosion of wartime collectivism and strong liberal tendencies within the social security system. Nevertheless, the Conservatives did put in place some supply-side approaches and institutions that were later built on by New Labour after 1997. These were initially provided through the Manpower Services Commission (MSC), a tripartite quango set up in 1973 as part of a wider initiative to 'modernise' the employment service through the 1973 Employment Training Act. A key feature of this Act was to create a more widely used and more customer-friendly service through the creation of 'self-service' job centres, separating employment search from benefit payment to reduce the stigma of the dole associated with 'labour exchanges'. At the end of the 1970s, this was much criticised on the grounds that it encouraged fraud and welfare dependency – notably by the economist Richard Layard, who later became a key architect of New Labour's welfare-to-work programme (Price, 2000, p 203). Ironically, it was Heath's Conservative government after 1970 that broke the long-standing fusion of the employment service and benefits provision.

The measures administered by the MSC in the 1980s included the introduction of compulsory training schemes for young people and the long-term unemployed through the Youth Training Scheme (YTS) and Employment Training (ET). Also significant was the development of an individual casework approach after 1985, inviting claimants to periodic Restart interviews at which 'back-to-work' plans were formulated. There were also belated efforts to improve training after 1980 through employer-led Training and Enterprise Councils (TECs) that later became refashioned into the Learning and Skills Council

(LSC). At the same time, plans were laid to integrate benefits offices and job centres and hive them off from the civil service to an employment service (King, 1995, p 192). The Conservatives' intentions were mixed: to reduce measured unemployment rates by transferring people to training schemes, to reduce benefit expenditure, to provide genuine help and reskilling and to compel unemployed people to enter into low-wage, often service, employment.

The reforms culminated in the Jobseeker's Allowance in 1996 that replaced Beveridge's Unemployment Benefit established in 1946. This was a key reform by the Major government, consolidating the shift to workfare by ending the historic distinction between rights-based contributory insurance benefits and conditional means-tested social assistance. Jobseeker's Allowance is paid to unemployed people deemed capable of work, who must be 'immediately' available and willing to work either full or part time in each week that they are claiming benefit. Claimants have to sign a 'jobseeker's agreement' and show that they are 'actively seeking work' by taking such defined 'steps' as writing letters, telephoning or visiting employers, preparing a CV and getting specialist advice or undertaking appropriate training. Failure to sign on or attend an interview can lead to loss of benefit. There is a range of sanctions involving loss of benefit for not taking up employment or for leaving a job without good cause (CPAG, 2006, chapter 15).

Materialist, idealist and political mobilisation approaches all provide insights into this significant reform. From a materialist perspective (Jessop, 1994), compulsory workfare is linked to the transformation from an industrial to a post-industrial (post-Fordist) economy, in which the power of the national state is reduced by globalisation. Since there is reduced scope to control the economy by national Keynesian demand-side intervention, the aim of policy is to facilitate or enforce participation in unattractive low-paid work. This approach is built on by Peck's (2001) analysis of the shift to 'workfare states', although he also gives substantial recognition to the role of politics and ideology in creating different national pathways. From the evidence of this chapter, however, Peck arguably exaggerates the difference between 'workfare' and previous 'welfare', which has been shown to have strong 'liberal' elements. Nevertheless, he shows how the decentralised approach and adaptation to local conditions come more to the fore within a supply-side framework, and this helps to provide an explanation of why 'post-Fordism' creates a significant role for economic CBIs. However, the state sets clear 'guidelines' and mechanisms to ensure an 'approved' range of strategies are followed. In Britain, the system of New Deals discussed below is in fact a strongly centralised system. Thus, Giddens offers an optimistic view that:

> ... globalisation has a 'push down' effect, promoting the local devolution of power and bottom-up community activism. (Giddens, 2000, p 63)

However, we argue that such activism is also subject to the constraining power of national government targeting regimes that seek to channel their influence to meet the perceived imperatives of globalisation, which has been amply illustrated by the case study chapters in this book.

The post-structuralist approach sees Jobseeker's Allowance and the subsequent New Labour policies that built on its foundation in terms of the development of 'technologies' concerned with 'governmentality' of claimants, that is, aiming to be more than merely repressive, seeking their willing and active participation in training and job search (Walters, 2000, chapter 6). This rightly highlights how a welfare gloss and community incorporation are necessary for mobilising consent, rather than a simple reliance on repressive power. Both materialist and post-structuralist approaches, however, seem to eliminate unemployed people as active subjects pursuing their own agendas, including resistance to welfare-to-work (Mizen, 1998). While strong materialist accounts do highlight the social causes of unemployment, they can engender a pessimism that there's not much that can be done to challenge the dictates of globalisation and post-industrial capitalism. In denying scope for significant political choice, they may unwittingly serve also as a *justification* for the shift to workfare. A critical realist approach can take account of strong economic pressures, but still leave scope for some optimism about the possibility of political choices, if collective agency can be mobilised (a case elaborated on in Chapter Eleven).

New Labour's mid-Atlantic economic and social policy

New Labour's economic and social policies have been built on the platform established by the Thatcher and Major governments within a longer-term liberal inheritance. They are designated mid-Atlantic, because although they share features of European human capital approaches, they increasingly emphasise a US-style work-first strategy.

As a result, although they made some progress in relation to their own targets and objectives, and from the standpoint of disadvantaged and excluded people, this stalled by the time of Labour's third term from 2005. As acknowledged by Diamond and Giddens:

> Inevitably, much of the progress made since 1997 has been achieved by plucking the 'low hanging fruit'. (Diamond and Giddens, 2005, p 109)

This is primarily because New Labour's economic policies provide the fundamental straightjacket within which the social policies must operate. This is characterised by Hay (2001, 2004) as neo-monetarist, involving a 'technicisation' or depoliticisation of economic policy, largely restricting it to the manipulation of interest rates to maintain low inflation, overseen by a semi-autonomous Bank of England. This is seen as essential to maintaining the overall health of the economy by maintaining an open international economy and a flexible labour market. It is claimed that this generated sustained economic prosperity that has helped to lower unemployment since the mid-1990s. In this model, the economy is seen as being freed to create jobs, which is not the government's responsibility. Social policy then intervenes on the supply side with sticks and carrots, compulsions and forms of support, to ensure take-up of the jobs created.

This strategy was the result of a political choice. At the end of the last Conservative era, there were calls by some for a shift to European 'stakeholder' capitalism, building over the long term for profitability, embracing a corporatist approach involving labour fully as a social partner, and a more redistributionist social policy (for example, Hutton, 1995). This did not happen. The influential 1994 OECD (Organisation for Economic Co-operation and Development) Jobs Study portrayed the European model as 'sclerotic', ostensibly preventing labour market flexibility and as a result protecting those within the labour market against those outside it. In power, New Labour has substantially imitated the US approach to the labour market to facilitate (i) short-term profitability, (ii) the creation of the maximum number of low-paid jobs and (iii) work-first social policies to ensure integration of marginalised members of society as citizen-workers. This has been claimed to be beneficial to those at the base in providing a 'stepping stone' to later labour market progression, although the supposed benefits of the US model in its home territory are disputed on economic efficiency and social justice grounds (for example, Herzenberg et al, 1998; Ehrenreich, 2001).

Under New Labour, Britain has undoubtedly shifted somewhat closer towards Europe, Thatcherite hostility giving way to a lukewarm if not enthusiastic approach. Labour immediately signed up to the European Social Chapter, adopted the European Charter on Human Rights (ECHR) into British law in 1998, and has largely followed European directives, for example, strengthening anti-discrimination legislation in the wake of the 2000 employment directives across the range focused on in this book. However, New Labour has challenged the European social model, promoting individual 'fitness' in the face of the market rather than social 'protection' against it. As Tony Blair put it in a speech to the European Parliament in 2005:

> The purpose of our social model should be to enhance our ability to compete, to help our people cope with globalisation, to let them embrace its opportunities and avoid its dangers. Of course we want a social Europe. But it must be a social Europe that works. (BBC News, Full text: Blair's European speech, 23/6/05)

Under the European Union's (EU's) 2000 Lisbon Strategy, there is undoubtedly a strong shift towards greater liberalisation, privatisation and pursuit of more flexible labour markets. However, this is combined with a notion of promoting a 'knowledge society' in which Europe competes by enhancing the skills and productivity of the workforce. This is (problematically) seen as compatible with modernising the European social model, promoting social inclusion, equality and solidarity, and avoiding a 'race to the bottom'. The Lisbon Strategy is thus more associated with a human capital rather than a work-first approach to 'labour activation' or welfare-to-work, aiming to enhance skills and ensure progression, rather than wholly focused on early integration into the labour market. It is thus compatible with a stronger role for what Giddens calls the 'social investment state', although this is often more an aspiration rather than a reality in the British context. In other words, the New Labour and Lisbon strategies represent somewhat different projects to politically construct what Elger and Burnham (2001), building on Cerny (1997), term a 'competition state' to respond to the perceived 'requirements' of globalisation. While Lisbon could be seen as allowing somewhat more scope for a stronger emphasis on social solidarity, the social is still subordinate to the economic, in ways that contrive to reduce the scope for democratic politics (Cerny, 1999).

New Labour's supply-side social policies have focused not just on reducing International Labour Organization (ILO) unemployment, which is behaviourally defined by the Labour Force Survey (LFS) in terms of those actively seeking work, but also on raising the employment rate generally and in relation to particular groups, beyond those required by the Lisbon Strategy. In other words, it focuses on the 'workless' conceptualised as both individuals and households. In principle, this appears a neutral, even inclusive, definition but in practice the supposed reluctance of the workless to engage in the labour market is seen as at best due to lack of confidence and often a wilful act, particularly in a tight labour market. In other words, behavioural traits are often attributed to those targeted. In 1997, Tony Blair talked of 'the new workless class', while in 2002 Gordon Brown promised a conference in Birmingham that the New Deal for Employment would be:

> ... an onslaught against the unacceptable culture of worklessness that grew up in some of our communities in the 1980s and early 1990s. (http://news/bbc.co.uk/1/low/uk_politics/2384437.stm)

This emphasis on behavioural traits within official worklessness discourse focuses on negative characteristics, especially people's lack of paid work, rather than their positive capabilities, including involvement in informal activity and unpaid work such as family responsibilities and various forms of involvement in local communities (Evans et al, 2006). Thus 'workless' is not a neutral but a heavily loaded term, and it serves also to justify the increasing resort to compulsion within the workfare state, if people are not proving willing to do what is deemed to be good for them, the economy and the Exchequer.

A brief audit of New Labour's employment policies

In its efforts to tackle unemployment and worklessness, the government has set ambitious employment rate targets. By 2004, it had met the EU's 2001 targets to raise the employment rate of those of working age generally to 70%, women's to 60% and older workers' (55-64) to 50% by 2010, and it set more of its own targets, also seeing these as essential to meet its child poverty targets: an overall target of 80%, a female rate of 65% and an older worker target of 56%. The Department for Work and Pensions also has targets to improve the employment rate of people living in disadvantaged areas and disabled people and an ambitious lone-parent employment rate target of 70% (DWP, 2006a). They have, as will be seen, been more successful in tackling ILO unemployment than reducing worklessness.

In developing these targets, the government has moved beyond the traditional male, able-bodied breadwinner model that placed rights and obligations to employment on some, and granted exemptions or enforced exclusions on others. However, in seeking to expand the 'rights' to employment through supply-side measures, it is not only tackling past exclusions, but also seeking to restrict or challenge previous 'privileged' exemptions. Thus the government's oft-stated policy of 'work for all those who can, security for all those who cannot' contains both promise and threat in varying degrees. There have undoubtedly been some successes for this strategy, with benefits to disadvantaged people and communities, although how much can be attributed to the general buoyancy of the economy or specific social policy measures is a matter of debate. When Jobseeker's Allowance was going through Parliament, Labour promised that it would be abolished. In practice, its active labour market policies have been built on the restrictive foundations of Jobseeker's Allowance. While public expenditure was generally restricted through New Labour's first term up to 2001, a £5 billion windfall tax was raised on the profits of privatised utilities to resource the New Deal for Young People (NDYP) and a series of allied initiatives for the over-25s, lone parents, disabled people and those over 50. This system was mainstreamed during Labour's second term, raising Britain's low expenditure on labour market measures compared with other industrialised countries, but it still remains one of the lowest spenders along with the US, consistent with a work-first approach offering only temporary support.

There were three key interventions that define this expanded supply-side approach: the national minimum wage (NMW), tax credits and the National Childcare Strategy aimed at 'making work pay'. In addition there were a range of community initiatives such as Employment Zones and other labour market experiments, as well as employment initiatives as part of community experiments such as the New Deal for Communities (NDC) and the Neighbourhood Renewal Fund (NRF) funding of regeneration schemes. There were also measures to 'modernise' the employment services and link them with the administration of benefits through Jobcentre Plus, launched from 2001, involving a self-service approach for mainstream users, so that employment advisers could concentrate more intensively on unemployed clients.

Of the additional measures the first, the NMW implemented in 1999, has been the clearest success. Initially set low, it has been raised by stages based on recommendations of a semi-autonomous Low Pay Commission. It has managed to do this without significantly affecting inflation or having discernible employment effects. From April 1999 to October 2006 the 'bite' in relation to the 60% median wage – the official poverty line – increased from 47.6% to 53% (Low Pay Commission, 2007, p 7). However, this is still seven percentage points short of the 60% 'decency threshold'. Under Gordon Brown, tax credits have become an increasingly important way of tempting parents into the labour market, with the aim of transforming Britain from a single to a 'dual breadwinner' state. Launched in 1999, they are administered by the Inland Revenue to maintain the pretence that they are not social security benefits. Revisions to the system in 2003 divided them into separate Child Tax and Working Tax Credits, claimable by those working 16 hours a week or more. Low-paid workers without children, if they work more than 30 hours a week, or 16 hours if disabled, can claim Working Tax Credit. Working Tax Credit includes a childcare element, including up to 80% of the costs of eligible childcare, linked to the National Childcare Strategy.

The National Childcare Strategy, launched in 1997, is part of New Labour's commitment to anti-poverty and 'family-friendly' policies, some of which are in response to European directives. For the first time the 2006 Childcare Act placed a responsibility on local authorities to work with partners to ensure sufficient childcare in their locality for working parents. However, a key problem not addressed is affordability, which creates barriers to employment participation, despite vouchers. According to the Daycare Trust survey, the average cost of a nursery place for a child under two was around £155 a week in January 2007 and higher in London and the South East. The government did increase free nursery places, including for those in training, as part of the March 2007 Budget, yet while countries like Denmark fund 70% of childcare costs, Britain only funds around 30% (Daycare Trust, 2006, 2007).

The New Deal programmes are the central policy, with most resources devoted to the NDYP, involving a 'gateway' where the benefits client is assessed by a 'personal adviser' and helped to decide between four options, a subsidised job with a regular employer, £15 on top of benefits for voluntary work or as a member of an environmental task force and full-time vocational training. A 'fifth option' of not working or being inactive is not available if benefits are to be retained. There are other New Deals including for adults over 25, older workers, lone parents and disabled people, with slightly different rules and degrees of compulsion. New Deals are work-first programmes essentially focused on developing employability skills and early entry into the labour market. A sustainable job is also defined in the short term as one held for three months or more. The programmes have been extensively evaluated according to these narrow criteria, and evidence (DWP, 2004) indicates modest success for the most employable on top of a buoyant labour market (Finn, 2001). Although broadly positive, however, the Trades Union Congress (2004) criticises the fact that up to a quarter do not sustain jobs for three months, and that Black and minority ethnic young people do not get as good a deal as White participants. They argue that local economic conditions play a significant part in degrees of success, and in high unemployment areas in the North there is considerable 'churning' or migration between short spells of work and benefit or training. At any one time, a large number of clients are in the gateway.

The government's general record on unemployment and worklessness against longer-term trends is presented in Table 10.1. This shows the ILO unemployment peaks of 1984 and 1993 under the Conservatives, and also how ILO unemployment overall has fallen under New Labour from 1997 back to, but not quite reaching, levels found in the early 1970s at the end of the postwar boom. This is a considerable achievement. In the early 1990s, many commentators were pronouncing the end of the era of full employment. The growth in employment rates is indicated in Table 10.2 and the UK rate is one of the highest for the G8 group of leading economies. It shows that women's employment increased faster than men's, continuing a trend that has mainly been upwards since 1971. The men's employment rates fell from 1971, when it was more than 90%, to reach its lowest point of 75% in 1993. Since then, it rose until 2000 and then levelled out, showing no signs of returning to the high levels of the early 1990s (ONS, 2006, p 20).

These trends have emerged in the context of rapid economic, demographic and social change. By mid-2005, there were 30.8 million jobs in Britain, one of the largest totals ever recorded. Public and private service sector jobs grew from 61% of the total in 1978 to 82% in 2005, with falls in manufacturing from 28% to 12% of jobs in this period (ONS, 2006, p 5). There was growth in both high- and low-paid jobs, and an increase in public sector employment since 1998, which had previously declined in the 1990s (ONS, 2006, p 26).

The general success in relation to ILO unemployment needs to be set against less impressive performance for particular groups. Men's unemployment rates have been consistently a percentage point higher than women's, and are higher among those under 24 years (ONS, 2006, pp 31-2). There are also significant ethnic differences shown for 2004 in Figure 10.1, with White rates at just under 5%, Indians

Table 10.1: Unemployment and economic inactivity for selected periods between 1971 and 2007, UK, seasonally adjusted

	Number ILO unemployed	% ILO unemployed	Total economic inactivity rate %	Male economic inactivity rate %	Female economic inactivity rate %
Jan-Mar 1971	980,000	3.8	36.8	16.4	55.3
Mar-May 1984	3,278,000	11.9	37.1	23.4	49.8
Dec-Feb 1993	3,027,000	10.7	37.1	26.7	46.8
Mar-May 1997	2,045,000	7.2	37.4	28.3	45.8
Nov-Jan 2007	1,692,000	5.5	36.5	29.1	43.4

Source: Adapted from ONS (2006), reproduced by permission

Table 10.2: Employment rate for men and women of working age (16 to 59/64), 1995 and 2005, UK

	All persons %	Men %	Women %
1995	71	76.5	66.1
2005	75	79.1	70.4

Source: ONS (2006, p 20)

higher, and Black Caribbeans and Pakistani/Bangladeshi people experiencing much higher rates. Ethnicity and gender also interact in complex ways. In most cases women's rates were lower than men's, but for Pakistani/Bangladeshi women, rates of ILO unemployment were over 19%, while Black Caribbeans experience the highest male rates. Rates of ILO unemployment are higher too among those in 'elementary' occupations compared with 'professional and managerial' occupations, and those with few skills or qualifications. Around one fifth of unemployed people have no qualifications. In other words, unemployment is strongly class-related. Poor health and disability – strongly class-related factors – are also associated with higher rates of unemployment. Around one fifth of unemployed people have a long-term health problem (ONS, 2006, p 33).

The factors associated with economic inactivity – ethnicity, class, qualifications, health and disability – are largely the same as those linked

Figure 10.1: ILO unemployment by ethnicity, men and women, 2004, Great Britain (%)

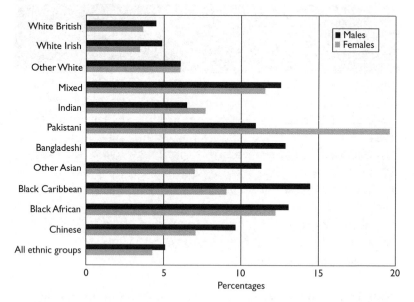

Source: ONS (2006), reproduced by permission

to higher rates of ILO unemployment. They are interconnected problems linked to structural disadvantage rather than simply behavioural issues, with severe class disadvantage often a common connecting thread. The figures in Table 10.1 show that overall economic inactivity rates have not altered much over the past three-and-a-half decades, but the composition has changed dramatically. While women's rates have fallen by nearly a fifth, men's rates have almost doubled, linked to a structural shift from an industrial to a post-industrial economy that has eliminated whole swathes of 'male' manufacturing employment, spinning older workers out, without providing attractive well-paid replacements for young men without qualifications. This has strong regional dimensions that have surfaced in many of the case study chapters. These spatial dimensions of political economic processes have under New Labour led, according to the Hetherington Commission (2006, pp 15-17), to even more rapid 'South-Easternisation' of the British economy, and the development of a huge city region of London and the congested 'Golden Arc' spreading in all directions around it, within which there are significant centres of deprivation and extreme polarisation of wealth and income, with low-waged service employment increasingly supplied by migrant labour. Further north and beyond are satellite city regions such as Birmingham, Manchester and West Yorkshire, and Central Scotland, which have developed knowledge and financial services sectors linked to the Golden Arc, and their own international linkages through local airports. However, these have been pictured as 'archipelagos' within seas of deprivation in which 'endogenous growth' – the favoured mechanism of government neo-monetarist economic policy – has not been able to generate sufficient new well-paid manual jobs to replace those lost by accelerating manufacturing decline.

The highest rates of worklessness – including ILO unemployment, inactivity generally, lone parents not working, excluded youth and people on Incapacity Benefit – are not surprisingly found in those areas that have been hit hardest by deindustrialisation, among people who do not have the means or capacity to compete within the emerging and highly polarised knowledge and services economy. This is not to deny that cultural and behavioural factors play some mediating role, but these are shaped by this wider environmental context, the effects of which government policies need to tackle. Government policies show only limited recognition of these forces, and the way that benefits trap severely disadvantaged people entering low-wage work. Instead most weight is placed on cultural and motivational influences, with 'welfare dependency' seen as a cause not a symptom of structural disadvantage. Although his name is no longer invoked, a modified version of Charles Murray's conservative and polemical claim that overgenerous 'welfare' gives rise to a self-perpetuating 'underclass' has strongly influenced the Labour Right through Frank Field, who served as Minister for Welfare Reform 1997-98 (for position statements from both, see Lister, 1996).

Economic restructuring linked to internationally successful commercial and ailing manufacturing sectors is not new (Gamble, 1994), but it has intensified with New Labour's political economy, through a strong currency that continues to weaken manufacturing exports, weak labour protection laws that make it easy for firms to migrate abroad and a booming housing market that reinforces regional barriers to mobility, and traps the most disadvantaged in run-down social housing with poor transport links to available jobs (Lupton, 2003). The government's figures show that economic inactivity rates are driven by complex factors, including the rise in the number of students of working age. There remains a division between those, primarily women, who are undertaking caring responsibilities for young children, and men, often in the older age groups, who have health problems and may be on either Severe Disablement Allowance or Incapacity Benefit (ONS, 2006, p 39). There have been some improvements in the direction desired by the government for some groups. For example, the numbers of single parents in employment, as shown in Figure 10.2, rose from just over 51% to 56.5% in the period 2001-06, although this remained substantially short of the government's 70% target rate, and still relatively low by international standards.

New Labour's policy plateau and the turn to greater compulsion

Despite the success in increasing overall employment levels, the New Labour government has increasingly recognised that its measures do not reach entrenched areas of unemployment and worklessness and it has sought new ways forward that depart from the proliferating and rather centralised set of New Deals. New initiatives have been based on working more closely with employers and contracting out to voluntary and private providers. The creation of an Adviser Discretion Fund allows for more flexible and sustained personalised programmes for those with 'multiple problems', including such innovations as work trials, in-work support and 'return-to-work credits' to subsidise people for the first year. This moves policy towards a more 'inclusive' approach favourable to the kinds of CBIs highlighted in preceding chapters of this book. Efforts to develop this into a more systematic

Figure 10.2: Lone parents in employment, 2001-06, Great Britain

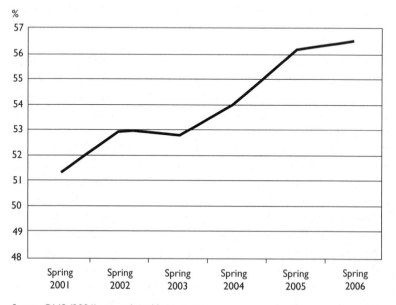

Source: ONS (2006), reproduced by permission

approach led to the Building on New Deal (BoND) proposals to find 'local solutions meeting individual needs' (DWP, 2004, p 16). Pathways to Work pilots were also developed for Incapacity Benefit clients and reportedly yielded promising results (Blyth, 2006).

Such initiatives potentially form the basis for improved, locally attuned and personalised supply-side interventions that can more effectively liberate people's individual agency. However, a structural analysis indicates that they would still need to be complemented by more sustained intervention on the demand side to improve the quality of jobs and to deal with the 'generative mechanisms' of labour market insecurity and inequality, which make vulnerable people even more vulnerable. The underlying assumptions of many welfare-to-work initiatives – that the majority of people are nearly job ready and that all that is required is a bit more employability in terms of general job skills and motivation – do not square with evidence of multiple barriers experienced by the most disadvantaged in the labour market (for example, Dean et al, 2003). This evidence triangulates with messages coming from the SEQUAL research into promising practices reported in the case study chapters. As will be recalled, project workers felt that they were having some success, but also complained that they were not given sufficient time with clients to tackle deep-seated problems, that benefit traps served as deterrents, people were not supported enough to gain jobs, and they were not able to support them within employment. Above all, respondents in the case study chapters drew attention to the need to improve the quality of jobs on offer in the labour market rather than just to provide more help to access those available.

This helps to explain why, during New Labour's third term, after 2005 a plateau had been reached in terms of positive effects for disadvantaged people, in terms of the government's own stated aims of reducing child poverty (Brewer et al, 2007) and tackling worklessness by getting greater numbers into paid employment. The implications of this are taken up in some detail in Chapter Eleven, but overall they indicate the need to tackle a range of inequalities, including class disadvantage, combining a structure–agency approach. Since 1997 government policies have placed very little emphasis on structural barriers. Instead they have been intensifying their supply-side, individual agency approach, while giving some recognition to the need for more intensive, longer-term and transitional support. However, the government is also turning increasingly to compulsion of workless people, seeing their problems as primarily due either to low morale or wilful resistance. Thus in an era when 'evidence-based policy' is supposed to hold sway government policies are at best selective about what evidence counts, at worst ignoring what is uncomfortable for it. Perhaps the government promotes this approach because it has decided it is not politically feasible to change structures, and in the absence of many positive incentives it needs to force people into the jobs that are available. It has also been mindful of concerns that migrants from EU accession countries may be starting to depress wage rates at the bottom, serving as a further disincentive to UK workless people to enter the labour market (Work and Pensions Select Committee, 2007).

'Welfare reform', as it is called, has been an enduring concern of New Labour since the late 1990s. Increasingly, the disciplinary approach initially applied to young people and older workers is being extended to more categories of claimants. Thus the Green Paper on welfare reform (DWP, 2006b) outlines government plans for 'empowering people to work' by combining greater support with increasing compulsion. There is an obvious contradiction, in that any meaningful concept of empowerment implies self-determination, including the right to decide whether paid work is advantageous or not for people's chosen life agendas, within or outside the labour market. This alternative approach to empowerment is at the heart of a capabilities and human rights approach elaborated on further in Chapter Eleven. The first outcome of the Green Paper is the 2007 Welfare Reform Act, which will abolish the current system of enhanced Incapacity Benefit rates for new claimants from 2008. The aim is to apply work-first principles by replacing Incapacity Benefit with a single Employment and Support Allowance that will be less generous, backed up by benefits sanctions. The Personal Capability Assessment of ability to work, acknowledged to be one of the toughest in the world, will be made even tougher (Preston, 2006).

The next stage in the 'welfare reform' process has been mapped out by the Freud Report (2007), commissioned by the Department for Work and Pensions, and broadly accepted by both the government and the Conservative opposition. For some, however, such as Frank Field (2007), its proposals are not tough enough. The Minister, John Hutton, in launching the review in December 2006, told an Institute for Public Policy Research conference that:

> The next challenge we face is to ensure the hardcore of 'can work but won't work' benefits claimants take advantage of the opportunities out there and compete for jobs alongside growing numbers of migrants who arrive in Britain specifically to look for work.... And for those who won't do so, there should be consequences, including less benefit

or no benefit at all. (www.cesi.org.uk/news/shownone. asp?nID=150)

Freud's central proposals for 'reducing dependency, increasing opportunity' focus on the money that would be saved by reducing the number of claimants. It recommends that the state employment service be confined to dealing with claimants in the early stages of unemployment, with subsequent contracting out of case management to private and voluntary sector providers to provide tailored, work-first assistance. It develops proposals to shift to a more outcome-focused approach over a three-year period in order to provide more intensive help for clients with multiple problems. This includes extending the principle of conditionality to lone parents, expecting them to work once their children have reached 12 years old. All of this is to be tested and rolled out over a six-year period. At the same time, it puts the case for a single unified benefit for those of working age to deal with the deterrent effects of over-complex benefits. The danger is that this will involve levelling down and not allow for individual circumstances.

The SEQUAL research does seem to indicate that unemployed people have often had negative experiences of the employment service, and the limited available evidence suggests that frontline staff may stereotype and underestimate the capacities of clients (for example, Wright, 2003). However, if the target-driven approach backed up by punitive sanctions were simply transferred elsewhere, to large-scale voluntary or private providers, similar problems are likely to recur. The evidence from many of the case study chapters is that the voluntary nature of the encounters is one of the most promising features of promising practices. Research conducted for the Public and Commercial Services Union (PCS), whose members work in the employment services, concludes that over-centralised and bureaucratic constraints on mainstream employment services are a problem, but that staff have been able to make a difference where they have been freed from them (Davies, 2006). There is certainly evidence from the case study chapters, for example Chapter Two on Coventry, that flexible, personalised services can be developed both within and outside the state sector, a key factor being the quality of relationships between providers and users and cooperative local partnership relations between organisations. After Brown became Prime Minister in June 2007 there were indeed signs of a cooling in enthusiasm for outright privatisation, with more emphasis on the role of local authorities (Tempest, 2007).

The Parliamentary Joint Committee on Human Rights (JCHR, 2007, pp 15-26) scrutinises legislation for its compatibility with the 1998

Human Rights Act, which is discussed in Chapter Eleven. It argued that the supportive elements of the (then) 2006 Welfare Reform Bill could enhance human rights, but questioned the increasing resort to compulsion, and delegating of sanctions to voluntary and private providers. Since the government acknowledges that nearly 9 in 10 people on Incapacity Benefit want to get back into work, one might query why compulsion and sanctions are necessary.

Conclusion: towards an evidence-based alternative?

This chapter has given due recognition to New Labour's achievement in expanding opportunities for employment, but has raised questions about whether its increasing resort to conditionality and compulsion is ethically justifiable and based on valid evidence concerning the causes of unemployment and worklessness. It has suggested that the refusal to challenge liberal traditions, and 're-politicise' economic policy and directly target inequality, leads to exaggerated expectations of the agency available to disadvantaged people. As well as the evidence already presented, the government's own analysis by the Social Exclusion Unit (2004) also disputed the 'welfare dependency' thesis. Instead it highlighted factors such as factory closures, 'residential sorting' in the housing market, 'place effects' such as poor transport and public services, and 'people effects' such as poor access to employment networks and employer discrimination. A research report for the Department of Communities and Local Government goes further and suggests that the problems arise outside households and neighbourhoods, and are the spatial consequences of the way that the shift from industrial to post-industrial capitalism is being managed – or rather not managed – in the UK. This leads to job losses in particular areas and also polarises society increasingly 'between relatively well paid professionals working in the knowledge industries, and low paid workers', with poor neighbourhoods aiding 'the production and reproduction of low cost labour' (North et al, 2006, p 3).

A justification of 'empowering' changes associated with the government's welfare reform programme is that they are needed to 'modernise' the benefits and welfare system. However, Wilkinson (2006) points out that the tax credit system involves elements of the 18th-century Speenhamland wage supplement system and the strict work tests echo the restrictive principles of the 19th-century Poor Law. It could also be added that low levels of benefits, uprated in line with prices rather than average earnings, have ensured that the Poor Law principle of 'less eligibility' has been the baseline from which New

Labour's 'making work pay' strategy has operated. The emphasis on individual case management as a way of patrolling the underclass, which has been a strong feature of welfare-to-work, was first pioneered by the voluntary sector through the Charity Organisation Society in the late 19th century, working in close alliance with local Poor Law Guardians. The shift away from the moralistic and individualist approach was central to the move to a modern welfare state (Harris, 2004). Therefore, if the proposals of the Freud Report (2007) are implemented, history may indeed have turned full circle.

However, while this chapter has sought to develop an evidence-based critique of current trends towards the workfare state, our book claims to explore policy possibilities beyond it. Despite their disagreements, contemporary materialist and post-structuralist approaches often seem to share a pessimism about whether 'another world is possible'. While New Labour seeks to compensate for its structural pessimism by emphasising individual agency, the analysis we seek to develop in Chapter Eleven raises possibilities for developing collective agency that might be facilitated by a shift to a capabilities and human rights approach.

References

Beveridge, W. (1942) *Social insurance and allied services*, Cmnd 6404, London: HMSO.

Blair, T. (2002) 'My vision for Britain', *The Observer*, 10 November.

Blyth, B. (2006) *Incapacity Benefit reforms – Pathways to Work pilots performance and analysis*, London: Department for Work and Pensions.

Brewer, M., Goodman, A., Muriel, A. and Sibieta, L. (2007) *Poverty and inequality in the UK*, Briefing note no 73, London: Institute for Fiscal Studies.

Calmfors, L., Forslund, A. and Hemström, M. (2001) 'Does active labour market policy work? Lessons from the Swedish experiences', *Swedish Economic Policy Review*, vol 85, pp 61-124.

Cerny, P.G. (1997) 'Paradoxes of the competition state; the dynamics of political globalisation', *Government and Opposition*, vol 32, no 2, pp 251-74.

Cerny, P.G. (1999) 'Globalisation and the erosion of democracy', *European Journal of Political Research*, vol 36, no 1, pp 1-26.

CPAG (Child Poverty Action Group) (2006) *Welfare benefits and tax credits handbook 2006/2007*, London: CPAG.

Davies, S. (2006) *Third sector provision of employment-related services: A report for PCS*, London: Public and Commercial Services Union.

Daycare Trust (2006) *Childcare today: A progress report on the government's ten-year childcare strategy*, London: Daycare Trust (www.daycaretrust.org.uk).

Daycare Trust (2007) *Childcare costs continue to rise beyond parents' reach*, Press release, London: Daycare Trust (www.daycaretrust.org.uk).

Dean, H., MacNeill, V. and Melrose, M. (2003) 'Ready to work? Understanding the experiences of people with multiple problems and needs', *Benefits*, vol 11, no 1, pp 19-25.

Diamond, P. and Giddens, A. (2005) 'The new egalitarianism: economic inequality in the UK', in A. Giddens and P. Diamond (eds) *The new egalitarianism*, Cambridge: Polity, pp 101-19.

DWP (Department for Work and Pensions) (2004) *Building on New Deal: Local solutions meeting individual needs*, London: DWP.

DWP (2006a) *Departmental report 2006*, London: DWP.

DWP (2006b) *A new deal for welfare: Empowering people to work*, London: DWP.

Ehrenreich, B. (2001) *Nickel and dimed: On (not) getting by in America*, New York, NY: Henry Holt.

Elger, T. and Burnham, P. (2001) 'Labour, globalization and the "competition state"', *Competition and Change*, vol 5, no 3, pp 245-67.

Esping-Andersen, G. (1990) *The three worlds of welfare capitalism*, Cambridge: Polity.

Evans, M., Syrett, S. and Williams, C. (2006) *Informal activities in deprived neighbourhoods*, London: Department for Communities and Local Government.

Field, F. (2007) 'Less carrot, more stick', *Daily Telegraph*, 6 March.

Finn, D. (2001) 'Modernisation or workfare? New Labour's work-based welfare state', *Competition and Change*, vol 5, no 3, pp 355-74.

Freud, D. (2007) *Reducing dependency, creating opportunity: Options for the future of welfare to work*, London: Department for Work and Pensions.

Gamble, A. (1994) *Britain in decline: Economic policy, political strategy and the British state* (4th edn), Basingstoke: Macmillan.

George, V. and Wilding, P. (1985) *Ideology and social welfare* (2nd edn), London: Routledge.

Giddens, A. (2000) *The third way and its critics*, Cambridge: Polity.

Harris, B. (2004) *The origins of the British welfare state: Society, state and social welfare, 1800-1945*, Basingstoke: Palgrave Macmillan.

Hay, C. (2001) 'Negotiating international constraints: the antimonies of credibility and competitiveness in the political economy of New Labour', *Competition and Change*, vol 5, no 3, pp 269-89.

Hay, C. (2004) 'Credibility, competitiveness and the business cycle in "third way" political economy: a critical evaluation of economic policy in Britain since 1997', *New Political Economy*, vol 9, no 1, pp 39-56.

Hetherington Commission (2006) *Connecting England: A framework for regional development*, London: Town and Country Planning Association.

Herzenberg, S.A., Alic, J.A. and Wial, H. (1998) *New rules for a new economy: Employment and opportunity in post-industrial America*, Ithaca, NY and London: ILR Press.

Hutton, W. (1995) *The state we're in*, London: Cape.

JCHR (Joint Committee on Human Rights) (2007) *Legislative scrutiny: First progress report*, Lords and Commons JCHR, Second report of session 2006-07, London: The Stationery Office.

Jessop, B. (1994) 'The transition to post-Fordism and the Schumpeterian workfare state', in R. Burrows and B. Loader (eds) *Towards a post-Fordist welfare state?*, London and New York, NY: Routledge, pp 13-37.

King, D. (1995) *Actively seeking work? The politics of unemployment and welfare policy in the United States and Great Britain*, Chicago, IL and London: University of Chicago Press.

Lewis, J. (1992) 'Gender and the development of welfare regimes', *Journal of European Social Policy*, vol 2, no 3, pp 159-73.

Lister, R. (ed) (1996) *Charles Murray and the underclass: The developing debate*, Choice in Welfare No 33, London: Institute of Economic Affairs.

Low Pay Commission (2007) *National Minimum Wage: Low Pay Commission Report 2007*, Cm 7056, London: The Stationery Office.

Lupton, R. (2003) *Poverty Street: The dynamics of neighbourhood decline and renewal*, Bristol: The Policy Press.

Mizen, P. (1998) '"Work-welfare" and the regulation of the poor: the pessimism of post-structuralism', *Capital and Class*, issue 65, pp 35-52.

North, D., Syrett, S. and Evans, M. (2006) *The economics of deprived neighbourhoods: Summary of research*, London: Department for Communities and Local Government.

ONS (Office for National Statistics) (2006) *Labour market review: 2006*, London: ONS.

Peck, J. (2001) *Workfare states*, New York, NY and London: The Guilford Press.

Preston, G. (2006) *A route out of poverty? Disabled people, work and welfare reform*, London: Child Poverty Action Group.

Price, D. (2000) *Office of hope: A history of the employment service*, London: Policy Studies Institute.

SEU (Social Exclusion Unit) (2004) *Jobs and enterprise in deprived areas*, London: SEU.

Tempest, M. (2007) 'Hain cools on the welfare-to-work privatisation', *The Guardian*, 31 July (http://business.guardian.co.uk/story/0,,2138607,00.htm#article_continue).

Tomlinson, J. (1994) 'British economic policy since 1945', in R. Floud and D. McCloskey (eds) *The economic history of Britain since 1700. Volume 3: 1939-1992* (2nd edn), Cambridge: Cambridge University Press, pp 255-83.

TUC (Trades Union Congress) (2004) *Labour market programmes*, London: TUC (www.tuc.org.uk).

Walters, W. (2000) *Unemployment and government: Genealogies of the social*, Cambridge: Cambridge University Press.

Wilkinson, F. (2006) 'Regimes of welfare and perceptions of the poor', Second Annual Stephen Lissenburgh Memorial Lecture, London: Policy Studies Institute (www.psi.org.uk/pdf/2006/WilkinsonLissenburghLecture.pdf).

Work and Pensions Select Committee (2007) *The government's employment strategy*, London: The Stationery Office.

Wright, S. (2003) 'The street-level implementation of unemployment policy', in J. Millar (ed) *Understanding social security: Issues for policy and practice*, Bristol: The Policy Press, pp 235-53.

ELEVEN

Capabilities, human rights and the challenge to workfare

Mick Carpenter and Stuart Speeden with Colin Griffin and Nick Walters

Beyond work-first and human capital approaches

This chapter builds on the critical appraisal of New Labour's labour market and social policies in Chapter Ten to point to possible futures 'beyond the workfare state'. It explores the kinds of measures that might be taken, involving more concerted efforts to tackle exclusion and disadvantage in genuinely empowering ways, to overcome the plateau effects occurring after 10 years of New Labour's work-first approaches.

The grounds for criticising this approach are, in part, social scientific, in that a greater awareness that the causes of unemployment and worklessness are due to the complex interplay of (social) structure and (personal) agency is likely to offer better, more strongly evidenced remedies. They are also political-ethical in that the resort to compulsion is a breach of human rights principles that is arguably likely to be ineffective or counterproductive. While claiming benignly to 'rebalance' rights with responsibilities, most of the latter are placed on disadvantaged people, with the government reluctant to date to shoulder some itself by intervening on the demand side to tackle structural inequalities and to improve the quality of jobs available.

A key question, however, is whether there are alternatives to current policies, which this final chapter therefore seeks to scope out, finding that some are being articulated within government circles, and some are being argued for externally by academics and think-tanks but they are also, we would emphasise, emerging out of the struggles by social movements from below. Thus it is in principle possible to envisage a future in which collective agency in civil society and the democratic sphere can be influential, and that we do not have to passively accept that the global market inevitably narrows possibilities for political choices. Our efforts to identify choices beyond the workfare state acknowledge that global economic pressures are significant, but can be mitigated by struggles around ideologies and discourse, and by the mobilisation of collective agency. While the strength of class-based movements may have weakened in the UK, the influence of new social movements claiming recognition and redress around the range of inequalities focused on in the case study chapters has grown. They are largely responsible for the pressure at local, European and global levels that in the UK has yielded the raft of anti-discrimination and positive equality duties that come together in the 2006 Equality Act, the implementation of which will be overseen by the Equality and Human Rights Commission (EHRC).

Placing emphasis on the role that collective agency must necessarily play does not mean denying the importance of struggle around discourse, and we therefore seek to identify a range of alternatives beyond current neoliberal economic and workfare social policies in the UK, within governments, universities, think-tanks and social movements. The most officially influential is the human capital approach that informs the Lisbon Strategy of competing globally by upgrading skills to create a high productivity, high-wage economy, rather than pursuing a race to the bottom where the 'comparative advantage' lies with poorer countries. This also underpins Giddens' (1998) notion of a 'social investment state'. It is sympathetic to the case for greater freedom and equality as long as it can be squared with the requirements of capitalist economic growth. It advocates more extensive supply-side intervention to upgrade skills, to improve economic productivity *and* facilitate progression in the labour market for disadvantaged groups. It is congruent with the 'business case' for promoting more equalities and diversity on the assumption that it improves business performance. This may sometimes be combined with a recognition that social considerations of greater equality need to be given greater consideration, often utilising the government's own emphasis on 'work–life' balance and the importance of parenting. Thus the important Harker (2006) report for the Department for Work and Pensions questions government efforts to cajole lone parents into any kind of work by arguing for a more supportive, parent-friendly 'work-first plus' approach, alongside substantial uprating of social security benefits, on the grounds that it is needed to meet the government's child poverty targets.

The obvious problem with a human capital or 'work-first plus' approach is that equalities measures are only seen as justifiable so long as they have an economic rationale consistent with current government policies. They therefore do not prioritise social or human rights considerations *over* economic considerations. Thus in the UK social security benefits are uprated in line with prices rather than earnings, after the Thatcher government in 1980 repealed the Rooker-Wise amendment to the Labour government's 1977 Finance Act. While from 2012 this may change for pensioners, there are no plans to do this for other claimants, due to government concerns that it might undermine work incentives for those of 'working age'. A radical social justice case for extending it to all might admit that it might well have this effect in enabling some people to pursue other priorities rather than be forced into low-paid work, but defend and celebrate it on these grounds.

Thus there are currently less mainstream but more radical alternatives beyond both the human capital critique of workfare linked to a capabilities and human rights approach. We identify two main emerging radical discourses: (i) 'egalitarian structuralist' approaches prioritising demand-side intervention to promote equality and 'better work' alongside an improved benefits system, within an employment-based society; and (ii) 'egalitarian utopian' approaches that promote a post-employment society encouraging informal community self-activity, often involving decoupling from the economic system. The four sets of policy discourses within and beyond workfare are summarised in Table 11.1 with the necessary caveat that the boundaries between different approaches are not always clear and there are also internal debates within as well as between discourses.

Our view is that the case study and wider evidence, while clearly indicating the limits of the work-first approach, is supportive of the idea that improvements can be made along human capital and work-first plus lines to current policies, that will substantially improve things from the standpoint of people who are disadvantaged and discriminated against. However, there is evidence supporting more radical alternatives, which can be analysed and clarified within the capabilities and human rights framework based on the work of Sen (1999) and extended by Nussbaum (2003). This argues that human needs and welfare are the chief objectives of public policy, and economic growth should be promoted only to the extent that it helps to expand human 'capabilities' including the freedom of people to act freely and autonomously, rather than just prioritising labour market participation, which places it in opposition to workfare. We link this to a broader conception of human rights encompassing both civil and political freedoms (for example, to work and not work) and economic, social and cultural rights (for example, to adequate social protection and rights to collectively organise). We agree with Sen (1999, p 3) on the centrality of labour rights to human rights:

Table 11.1: Summary of future economic and social policy strategies within and beyond the workfare state

Relation to workfare state	Labour market perspective	Policy approach
Within workfare	Any work is better than none – intensify	Work-first and compulsion within current supply-side approach
	A better and productive workforce required – modify	Human capital skills enhancement – more supply-side support and investment, plus economically justifiable equalities policies
Beyond workfare	Prioritise better work – transformative	Structuralist egalitarian – demand-side interventions to improve formal economy, alongside strong redistributive and equalities policies
	Post-employment – decoupling	Utopian egalitarian – support informal activity, eg subsistence-level minimum income

> Given the central – indeed unique – importance of labour power as an endowment for much of humanity, it is crucial to pay attention to the operation of labour markets.

To us this implies that class-based injustice must be tackled alongside other inequalities, and this also means resolving a tension in Sen's approach favouring both economic growth and social considerations. This means that a consensus on the promise of a capabilities and human rights approach must also leave scope for debate and disagreement on how to reconcile these and other tensions in terms of the political possibilities Table 11.1 identifies 'beyond workfare'.

The remainder of this chapter therefore follows the agenda through from proposals to modify workfare by human capital to examine proposals and initiatives that start to move beyond it. The capabilities and human rights frame is then analysed in some depth, developments in UK equalities and human rights chartered, and the chapter concludes with a discussion of emerging capabilities and human rights approaches linked to European social policy debates and the UK Equalities Review (2007).

Emerging UK strategies within and beyond workfare: human capital and more utopian alternatives

Chapter Ten acknowledged New Labour's achievements but also showed that behind the façade of low ILO (International Labour Organization) unemployment rates and general economic prosperity, widespread poverty and extreme inequality remain, and significant numbers of people experience difficulty accessing the labour market. The human capital critique argues that these are not the necessary corollaries of economic success but the symptoms of underlying competitive weaknesses. This, drawing on Hay (2004), provides some support for 're-politicising' economic policy, to address the UK's relatively poor productivity record, and to tackle inequalities by improving skills and rewards. This has been given impetus by the publication of the Leitch Report (HM Treasury, 2006), which states that the UK has been relatively good at turning out more graduates, but relatively poor in advancing basic and intermediate skills. Improving this situation is seen as key to improving the UK's underlying economic weakness and in addressing poverty, worklessness and social exclusion. The limitations of this strategy are set out in a Demos 'provocation paper' (Knell et al, 2007), which argues that Leitch's recommendations may well benefit those who are already skilled, and questions whether employers are the best arbiters of what training is provided. It proposes instead a partnership approach and casts considerable doubt on the continuing reliance on supply-side measures, implying that stronger employer compulsion and demand-side intervention are required (see also Lloyd and Payne, 2002).

The current reliance on neoliberal economic and workfare social policies is based on the assumption that welfare dependency undermines people's willingness to work. However, this is often contradicted by research, for example, showing that people from a range of White and minority ethnic groups with long-term health problems are often strongly motivated by the work ethic, although they may not necessarily give this absolute priority over family or community responsibilities (Salway et al, 2007). The government is seeking to strengthen families and communities, and has, as we saw in Chapter Ten, developed some relevant supportive social policies. However, it does not appear to accept that people's life goals may at times conflict with a 'work-first' strategy.

Advocates of a post-employment society argue that there needs to be more positive social recognition given to informal work to fulfil family and communal responsibilities. One study by Evans et al (2006) did acknowledge that such work played a key role in 'self-provisioning' in disadvantaged neighbourhoods, undertaken particularly by women, although it drew attention to what they called the 'negative' features of illegal paid work. However, a study by Katungi et al (2006) suggested that to regard the latter as always 'fraud' was not helpful, as people were often driven towards it by inadequate benefits, low wages and high childcare and housing costs. To some extent these issues can be dealt with at the edges of the current system although to deal with their implications more fully might require a radical shift from the current 'low pay' or 'no pay' system. For example, the Commission on Social Justice (1994) tentatively suggested that the strict availability for work rules might be relaxed to enable people to undertake education, training, voluntary and community work, parenting or other approved activities.

Another move a little further down towards the 'egalitarian utopian' road might acknowledge the implications that immediate employability is not feasible for those experiencing severe disadvantages. Thus Peck and Theodore (2000) identify some moves towards a social economy approach through the development of intermediate labour market (ILM) initiatives. To date, government-supported ILMs have mostly developed as community-based initiatives (CBIs) to help the most disadvantaged long-term unemployed people back into employment. They offer sheltered but 'real' paid work on a temporary basis, often up to a year, combined with support and training to enhance employability and job search. They tend to be found in the older industrial areas where they serve a range of social needs, such as childcare, IT (information technology) services and environmental work, resourced by European funding, New Deals or regeneration resources. They are typically administered by a voluntary third sector organisation. One of the key features is that participation is voluntary, distinguishing ILMs from workfare. Evaluations of ILMs indicate that they have had some success, although their work is often frustrated by paperwork requirements, and uncertainty about whether serving community needs should be seen as valid in itself or a temporary expedient before a 'proper' job (Finn and Simmonds, 2003).

A more radical alternative might thus be to give permanent priority to community needs as part of a wider vision of a post-industrial, 'post-work' utopian future. This could potentially connect with advocacy of a subsistence-level citizen's minimum income divorced from work requirements, as proposed by Gorz (1999), which he also links to redistribution and improved social provision. Post-work strategies have involved 'green' experiments on the ground seeking to realise a future beyond global capitalism and the power of the multinationals, favouring decoupling strategies. One of these is LETS (Local Exchange Trading Schemes), involving local non-monetary exchanges of informal work through a local register or 'time bank', advocated as the germ of an alternative, more humanistic and environmentally sustainable social order, for example, LETSLINK UK (www.letslinkuk.net/). Levitas (2001) argues that, while for the foreseeable future an alternative to global capitalism is not feasible, it is still important to be 'against work' and to challenge the current New Labour orthodoxy that views it as a moral as well as economic imperative. She argues that much 'socially necessary labour' occurs outside the market, and much formal labour is not socially necessary and is demeaning and socially destructive. New Labour policies also contain a 'contradiction between the emphasis on paid work, and the equal emphasis on the importance of parenting and of community, both of which depend on unpaid labour' (Levitas, 2001, p 454). In a period where the increased activity of the formal economy is fostering global warming and threatening planetary sustainability, the arguments for a radical decoupling from multinational consumer capitalism are gaining strength (for example, Monbiot, 2006).

Utopian strategies are demonstrating practical impact with potential wider implications in the long term. In giving value to non-economic activities and informal work, there exist ways of making it compatible with a capabilities and human rights approach. They can be criticised for not addressing the need to improve people's situation in the existing formal economy, by turning their back on efforts to improve it. This next section of the chapter therefore focuses on the problem of growing class-based inequality, and the prospects of transforming the formal economy and labour market.

Growing class-based inequality and emergence of transformative possibilities

The clear evidence is that 10 years of New Labour has only led to modest improvements in poverty, and made hardly any inroads into class-based economic inequalities. As Lawson (2006) point out, if Tony Blair's avowed aim was 'to take class out of British politics' its stubborn persistence through labour market and other distributive mechanisms makes it a continuing policy issue. Now that the Blair era is over, the possibility of at least a debate around these issues has opened up.

As far as relative poverty is concerned, the modest progress made during the first two terms of New Labour, linked to rising employment, tax credits and expansion of childcare, has stalled and even slightly reversed since 2004/05. The risk of falling into relative poverty, defined as 60% of the median wage after housing costs (AHC), fell modestly from 19.4% to 17.6% (Brewer et al, 2007, p 2). The Institute for Fiscal Studies analysis suggest that extra spending of £4 billion would be required to meet the government's 10-year target of reducing child poverty by half by 2010 (Brewer et al, 2007, p 2) at a time when the Treasury is seeking to rein in public expenditure.

As far as income inequality is concerned, the story is of a deliberate widening during the Thatcher years, through reductions in progressive taxation to make Britain one of the most unequal industrialised countries in the world. It continued to widen in New Labour's first term, and fell back somewhat after 2001, but by 2005/06 was more or less back to where it was in 1997, as measured by the Gini coefficient (Figure 11.1). Around three quarters of the extra income generated since 1997 has gone to richer households, although there has been some narrowing of gender inequality (Palmer et al, 2006).

One feature of New Labour is its emphasis on equality of opportunity rather than outcome, often measured in terms of intergenerational mobility, where there is also little evidence of improvement. At a time

Figure 11.1: Gini coefficient for equivalised disposable income (%)

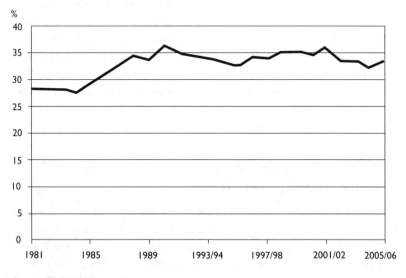

Source: ONS (2007), used by permission

when middle-class occupations have expanded, and typically require educational and professional qualifications, the children of the middle class have maintained a strong competitive advantage. Thus, Blanden et al (2005) show that Britain and the US remain significantly less mobile than Canada and the Nordic countries. Mobility actually fell in the 1980s and although more poor children stayed on in education, inequalities in access to higher education widened. It is predicted that recent funding changes in higher education are likely to widen inequalities further. A limitation of this study is that it used the conventional approach in defining mobility in terms of sons' destinations. As far as gender is concerned, a review by Dex et al (2005) shows that women are combining employment and mothering to a greater extent than in the past, and taking shorter breaks, and returning to their same jobs, whereas in the past, it was much more likely to lead to downward mobility. Maternity provisions have undoubtedly facilitated this. Women have also been closing the pay gap with men, and have lower ILO unemployment rates. However, achievement in the labour market is closely linked to class and ethnicity, and progress is therefore uneven. For many working-class mothers, work is part time and such jobs are often more insecure, poorly paid and offer few prospects for promotion (DCLG, 2007).

As far as 'race' and class is concerned, investigation by the Equal Opportunities Commission showed that Pakistani, Bangladeshi and African-Caribbean women experienced higher rates of unemployment, low pay and poorer promotion prospects, and the Department for Work and Pensions' Ethnic Minority Employment Taskforce is seeking to find ways of addressing these issues. Evidence on opportunity and ethnicity (Platt, 2005) shows that the first generation experienced downward mobility (as is happening to more recent migrants, see Chapter Nine, this volume), while their children often experience a compensating rise, often associated with educational attainment. However, there are exceptions, in that second-generation Pakistanis still tend to experience downward mobility (Platt, 2005). As both Chapters Four and Ten showed, there is a continuing ethnic penalty in the labour market for many people from minority ethnic groups (see also Clark and Drinkwater, 2007).

So far, the focus has been on income inequality but there are even more pronounced and growing inequalities in wealth. According to Beresford (2007) the 2007 *Sunday Times* 'rich list' shows that the period since 1997 'has proved a golden age for the rich, rarely seen in modern British history'. Some have argued that this situation of runaway wealth necessitates a shift from income tax to taxes on assets, including land, as a means of creating resources for redistribution, and taking some of the heat out of the housing market. In 2007, the Liberal Democrats proposed a wealth tax on homes worth £1 million or more (Temko, 2007). One of the most controversial areas has been highly visible city bonuses, £21 billion being paid out in 2006, with Goldman Sachs alone giving £8.3 billion to 4,000 of their workers, who each received £1 million or more (I-UK, 2007). Of Britain's marketable wealth in 2003, the wealthiest 10% owned 53% if housing is included and 71% if it is excluded. By contrast the bottom 50% owned 7% if housing is included, and 1% if it is not (ONS, 2006).

These inequalities are not incidental but integral to the operation of labour markets and wider political economic processes. Recent research shows that the effects of the government's liberalisation, flexibilisation and 'South-Easternisation' of the economy and society has created an 'hourglass' labour market in which, outside the super rich, many people have prospered and maintained their security, but there is a bulging group at the base who are falling behind and who face unenviable work prospects (Nolan, 2004). This leads, according to Goos and Manning (2003), to increasing polarisation between 'lousy and lovely' jobs. Research conducted by the Policy Studies Institute for the Trades Union Congress (TUC) estimates that one in five workers, in particular agency workers, migrant workers, informal workers and homeworkers, are in a 'vulnerable' situation and often denied their basic rights (Hudson, 2006), This could be understood as extreme class disadvantage, compounded by other forms of structural disadvantage based on gender, 'race' and nationality. Research for the Joseph Rowntree Foundation has shown that on the 200th anniversary of the abolition of the slave trade, 'modern slavery' is flourishing in the UK (Craig et al, 2007). Donovan (2006) argues that the estimated half-million or more undocumented migrant workers, many of them failed asylum seekers, have had their benefit cut off, have been denied healthcare and the right to work and to pay taxes. This is occurring at a time when the government is seeking to compel other groups of workers *into* the labour market.

These examples show how, at the bottom end, a flexible labour market can operate in ways that flout basic human rights; even in an advanced and prosperous economy, these are extreme examples of the way in which an open global economy creates both winners and losers. For the losers, weak economic and social rights are compounded by the weakened role of trade unions as a source of protection and influence, reinforced by the draconian legislation of the Thatcher era. New Labour has only tinkered with this, for fear it will discourage internal investment, in ways that still flout a number of important ILO conventions (Smith and Morton, 2006). A plausible case can be made to address these on both human capital and wider social justice grounds, that improving labour rights and stronger measures to tackle low income will help to address the UK's productivity problem. This might be most effective if combined with effective demand-side intervention to create greater stability in the labour market, encouraging investment in workers and improved management methods.

To this end, there are emerging campaigns from below to improve the quality of jobs available in terms of pay, security and decent treatment and progression, for example, the TUC's efforts to get unions working together effectively to tackle the problems experienced by vulnerable workers through the Working on the Edge campaign (Hudson, 2006, p 19). The TUC has campaigned for a Trade Union Freedom Bill to remove the straightjackets on unions taking industrial action, as unions today have fewer rights in this regard than at the beginning of the 20th century (TUC, 2006). A further campaign has been mounted to implement the draft European Union (EU) Temporary Agency Workers Directive that aims to create parity between temporary and permanent staff in pay, leave entitlements and other benefits. The government has so far declined to accept this on the grounds that it would backfire against workers and lead to less temporary employment. For this reason, it did not allow a Private Member's Bill, tabled by Paul Farrelly MP in March 2007, to ensure equal treatment for Britain's 1.4 million agency workers to progress (T&G News, 2007). A campaign has also been launched by the National Group on Homeworking (2006) to implement the 1996 ILO Convention on Homework, which set standards for minimum employment rights, including parity with other wage earners. Despite the formal commitment to 'work–life' balance, the government continues to resist the implementation of the EU Working Time Directive and the 48-hour week (Hollingshead, 2006).

While the government continues to argue that 'work is the best and most sustainable route out of poverty' (John Hutton, cited in ePolitix, 2006), this does not take account of the fact that any foothold in the labour market for the most disadvantaged is often precarious. Around half the men and one third of the women making a new claim for Jobseeker's Allowance in 2004/05 were last claiming less than six months previously and these proportions have not changed since 1997 (Palmer et al, 2006, p 79). Second, and more significantly, paid work does not always lift people out of poverty, as around half of both adults and children in poverty in 2004/05 were in households where someone was in work (Palmer et al, 2006, p 43). Attempts to remedy this from below have sought to campaign locally for a 'living wage' in contrast to the government's 'making work pay' strategy. In the UK this has been notably pursued by an alliance of churches and trade unionists through The East London Communities Organisation (TELCO) (Wills, 2004). Such campaigns are undoubtedly compatible with a capabilities and human rights approach, alongside campaigns for a living income. We therefore turn now to define and discuss this approach and how it might then inform policy in the UK.

Developing a capabilities and human rights approach to labour market inequalities

The capabilities approach: key features and internal debates

The basic feature of the capabilities approach is that all human beings have essentially similar needs and potentialities, and that there is therefore a moral and political responsibility on human rights grounds to respect these and actively create the economic, social and political conditions through which people can 'flourish' and achieve 'personhood' (Sen, 1999; Nussbaum, 2003). Its emphasis on freedom and democracy means that people must be empowered to decide what is in their best interests. It also recognises that people are not equally placed to realise their human capabilities, through gender, 'race', disabilities and other structured inequalities, and therefore political action is required to tackle these and to enable it to happen.

For all these reasons, we see a capabilities approach as consistent with the messages coming from the SEQUAL research and the wider evidence considered in the last two chapters. These include the best or most promising features of employment CBIs, namely a holistic and humanistic approach in which all needs and aspirations are addressed, rather than simply focusing on getting people into employment at all costs. It fundamentally involves a collaborative approach between providers and users, whether within or outside the state sector, in which efforts are made to put people in reach of employment, and where necessary to encourage them to consider and strive for it: it should also be recognised, however, that employment may not universally be the best option, and that people must ultimately be left to decide for themselves. Some incipient characteristics of this approach are present within the case study chapters, but there is also a recognition of the limits of the community-based approach and agency within prevailing policies. In many ways, we would argue, practitioners working with employment CBIs have implicitly been working with a capabilities outlook, sometimes giving it a different name (for example, the social model of disability). Making it explicit across the range of welfare interventions would, we believe, help to clarify and enhance this further, and also provide the means for a more concerted challenge to workfare.

The basic conceptual and working ideas of the capabilities approach are simple enough, with economic and public policy seen as 'a process of expanding the substantive freedoms that people have' (Sen, 1999, p 297). Capabilities are defined as human 'functionings' within and outside the formal economy and labour market, and include what people 'value doing or being' as well as observable 'achieved functionings' such as literacy, life expectancy and so on. Sen's concept of 'complex' as well as 'basic' capabilities identifies the need to address the 'shame' that excludes people from the public sphere, which he links to gender, but which could be extended to issues of sexuality, mental illness, physical ill health, disability and other inequalities. Sen explicitly sees the concept of human capital as insufficient, although he still calls it 'enriching' and in need of 'supplementation':

> This is because human beings are not merely means of production, but also the end of the exercise. (Sen, 1999, pp 295-6)

This therefore expresses ambiguity about the capitalist market and economic growth, with little discussion about how class-based inequality might impinge on limiting human freedoms and potentialities. He has also been criticised for focusing too exclusively on individual capabilities, with insufficient allowance given for collective self-help from below and provision of 'public goods' from above (Evans, 2002; Ibrahim, 2006). Some critics have also argued for a participative approach to identifying needs and capabilities, for example, Clark (2005), who has sought to implement this in a South African context (Clark, 2003). There is clearly a tension here between top-down and bottom-up approaches to defining human freedoms and capabilities, which, to some extent, involves political differences that require further discussion and debate.

Human rights in the global arena: three waves of political struggle

There is extensive debate about whether the grounds for human rights are ethical, political or sociological. The position taken here is that they are a combination of all three and, in this, the capabilities approach is similar to other frameworks such as human needs theory (Doyal and Gough, 1991), and the social model of disability endorsed earlier in Chapter Three. However, given our theoretical standpoint, and our endorsement of a participative approach to defining and realising capabilities, emphasis needs to be given to seeing human rights as shaped by political mobilisations from different groups, seizing advantage of particular political 'moments'.

In this regard Klug (2005) identifies three waves of human rights, although our interpretation of the influences on them adds somewhat to hers. The first wave, around the time of the North American and French revolutions, she sees as linked to efforts to remove arbitrary rule of states and religious leaders. We would also see it as due to the efforts of the disenfranchised middle class to assert their power in a disintegrating feudal society. The key theorist in this regard was John Locke, whose pre-social conception of 'natural rights' of the free individual included property rights, which became subject to a socialist critique by Marx and others (Roth, 2004). The second wave of human rights Klug sees as occurring at the end of the Second World War in response to the horrors of war, Nazism and subsequently the Gulag. It gave rise to the 1948 United Nations Declaration of Human Rights (UNDHR), out of which the European Convention on Human Rights (ECHR) also flowed. We would add that it was also in response to the socialist critique and mobilisations of the labour movement, which led to the extension of the notion of human rights from 'negative' human freedoms to civil and political rights, to positive conceptions of substantive 'economic, social and cultural' rights to a decent material life. The Cold War unfortunately led these being separated, with the prime emphasis being primarily placed on civil and political rights in the West, and economic, social and cultural rights seen as secondary.

Klug sees the third wave of human rights as occurring after 1989, with the fall of the Berlin Wall and the end of state socialism. She sees it as removing the obstacle to reintegrating civil and political and economic, social and cultural rights, alongside a stronger emphasis on participation and development of civil society. We would argue that this third wave is in fact associated with contradictory tendencies. On the one hand, the defeat of state socialism and triumph of neoliberalism has led to a reassertion of civil and political rights as the prime meaning of human rights. On the other, an alliance of labour interests, new social movements and human rights activists have combined to seek to counter the tendency of global capitalism and transnational corporations to exercise arbitrary power and undermine civil and political and economic, social and cultural rights (Johnson, 2004).

Although the capabilities framework has been developed independently of human rights discourses, there is no doubt that the two are closely allied (Vizard, 2006). Indeed the capabilities approach could be seen as a political as well as intellectual product of the third wave seeking to provide sound social scientific reasons for asserting the indivisibility of civil and political and economic, social and cultural rights, against neoliberal efforts to separate them.

The politicisation of equalities and human rights in the UK

These become important policy issues given the incorporation of the Council of Europe's ECHR into UK law through the 1998 Human Rights Act. In addition, under pressure from Europe, there has been a raft of legislation covering the range of inequalities, gender, 'race', disability, sexuality, age, religion and political belief examined in the case study chapters – with the notable exception of social class. Following the creation of the EHRC in the wake of the 2006 Equality Act and the forthcoming Single Equality Act to rationalise and integrate anti-discrimination legislation, the UK is acknowledged as having the most developed equalities framework in Europe.

According to McLaughlin (2007), this has led to a dual 'equality' system in the UK, one through the welfare state and the other through anti-discrimination legislation. Attention therefore needs to be given to seeing how they can work together, and, from this book's perspective, the possibilities thereby of moving beyond the workfare state. In this regard the endorsement of the capabilities and human rights approach by the Equalities Review (2007) has potentially far-reaching implications in terms of advancing the cause that economic, social and cultural rights should also be enshrined in UK law. Nevertheless McLaughlin (2007) argues that although there are moves to introduce 'positive' duties in the field of gender, 'race' and disability, the system is still concerned with tackling breaches once they occur, and the Human Rights Act itself is primarily concerned with civil and political rights within a Council of Europe framework that was established over 50 years ago, covering, among other things, the following rights:

Article 2: right to life
Article 3: protection against torture
Article 4: freedom from slavery and forced labour
Article 5: protection against arbitrary arrest or detention

Article 6: right to a fair trial

Article 7: rights against retrospective criminalisation

Article 8: right to privacy

Article 9: freedom of thought, conscience and religion

Article 10: freedom of expression

Article 11: freedom of assembly

Article 12: right to marry

Article 13: right to an effective remedy where rights or freedoms are violated

Article 14: prohibition of discrimination (Hoffman and Rowe, 2006, pp 357-65).

There are occasions when civil and political rights can 'spill over' into issues of economic, social and cultural rights, for example, when lack of sufficient provision of government resources interferes with rights to privacy in an institutional setting. This legislation places a duty on public authorities, but not the private and voluntary sector.

Economic, social and cultural rights are covered by a separate 'Social Charter' of the Council of Europe first issued in 1961 and revised in 1996 covering health, housing, education, employment, legal and social protection, movement of persons and non-discrimination (Council of Europe, 2004). In addition the EU's Charter of Fundamental Rights covering both civil and political and economic, social and cultural rights appeared in 2000. This became part of the draft EU Constitution that by 2007 had yet to be adopted. However, the UN Covenant on economic, social and cultural rights produced in 1966, ratified by the UK in 1976, does include rights such as:

> Articles 6-9: right to work, fair remuneration, healthy working conditions, social security, collective bargaining and the right to strike

> Articles 10-13: social rights such as an adequate standard of living, housing, health and education, and special protection for mothers, children and young people

> Article 15: cultural rights and rights to enjoy benefits of scientific progress. (Ruxton and Karim, 2001, p 39)

The government claims that its welfare-to-work and other social policies are consistent with the Covenant. However, the UN Committee on economic, social and cultural rights, while praising the introduction of the Human Rights Act, suggested in 1999 that the UK government was in breach of the Covenant, particularly in relation to the absence of a legal right to strike, and the fact that workers can be legally dismissed for simply striking. The Committee has also been critical of the extent of poverty and widening inequality gaps in UK society, alongside a wide range of other issues (Ruxton and Karim, 2001, pp 40-1).

What this all indicates is that human rights have become an increasingly contested political field. At a time when some Labour politicians and the Conservative opposition are challenging the limited civil and political rights that exist in the wake of 9/11 and 7/7, and emphasise responsibilities over social rights, others such as Oxfam GB and JUSTICE are pressing for the extension of the legal protection of economic, social and cultural rights. They also argue that the existence of some economic, social and cultural rights in law, such as the national minimum wage (NMW) and equal pay for equal value, provides a challenge to the view that economic, social and cultural rights are 'non-justiciable' or not capable of being decided on in court. Some countries like South Africa and India have demonstrated this and constitutionally embedded these rights, including labour rights (Ruxton and Karim, 2001, pp 2-3, 16). Consistent with a capabilities and human rights approach, they argue that poverty and social exclusion, and the lack of effective voice often associated with them, are a 'denial of fundamental human rights' (Ruxton and Karim, 2001, p 7). Support for the extension of the Human Rights Act to cover economic, social and cultural rights received a boost through the 21st Report of the Parliamentary Joint Committee on Human Rights (2004), which recommended that, without undermining parliamentary sovereignty, a case existed for incorporating guarantees of UNESC Covenant rights in domestic law, and proposed that this should be taken forward by the EHRC in collaboration with the government.

There is no doubt that the most radical features of the new equalities system is the emergence of positive public duties to promote gender and 'race' equality that is also being extended to disability. The logic of the forthcoming Single Equality Act is to make this universal across the recognised forms of inequality, and will potentially facilitate an integrated, multidimensional and intersectional approach. The varying Codes of Practice associated with the duties start to map out how this might happen, the one for disability particularly emphasising the role of participation from below in ways that the others might emulate.

In the absence of similar duties, action in the private sector is often promoted in terms of the 'business case' for equality and diversity. This undoubtedly has some purchase but it cannot always be assumed that social justice will never have a price tag, and, as McLaughlin (2007) argues, there is a danger that discrimination will be seen as justifiable if it cannot be shown to have benefits for business. In fact, available research from the US does not show a clear relationship between diversity policies and business performance (Kochan et al, 2003). Diversity strategies in the UK are embryonic and more a feature of large firms like Sainsbury's, B&Q and the Nationwide Building Society, whereas, in 2005, 58.7% of UK employment was in the small and medium-sized enterprise (SME) sector (DTI, 2006).

At the time of writing, the potential application of the Human Rights Act to contracted-out public services remains a legally contested area. However, this does not prevent public agencies from using their powers of procurement to pursue equality and social objectives. This has been done widely in the US, Canada and South Africa. While its use in the UK is curtailed by the EU's competition rules on the Single Market there is some scope for applying social objectives, but this approach challenges the neoliberalism of New Labour. Orton and Ratcliffe (2005) argue that New Labour's adherence to a neoliberal political economy has limited the scope of procurement activity in tackling racial inequality and the 'ethnic penalty' in the labour market.

The impact of devolution on human rights approaches

There are a number of promising examples of equality regimes on which to draw in developing positive and proactive approaches. Internationally, these include the affirmative action and employment diversity strategies on 'race' and gender pursued in the US in response to the civil rights and feminist movements. The post-apartheid South African example in seeking to incorporate both civil and political and economic, social and cultural rights in the constitution has provided an important landmark in the development of constitutional rights. It has helped to influence the emergence of stronger 'rights' cultures than in England that have emerged in Scotland, Wales and Northern Ireland (McLaughlin, 2007). The most advanced institutional framework and culture was established in Northern Ireland in the wake of the 1997 Good Friday Agreement that pioneered the Equality Commission approach and the implementation of public sector duties. Northern Ireland also pioneered a 'fair employment' model from 1972, the only place in the UK where anything along the lines of the US 'affirmative action' approach has occurred. Even so, McLaughlin (2007, p 114) argues that the results have been mixed.

Nevertheless, Northern Ireland has the most advanced equalities regime in the UK, which can be largely traced to mobilisations from below by a civil rights movement in the 1960s. The Northern Ireland Human Rights Commission (NIHRC, 2001) has proposed incorporating both civil and political and economic, social and cultural rights in a Bill of Rights, drawing on the UN ESC Covenant and the EU Charter of Fundamental Rights, which would include a 'right to work'. There is considerable public support, in that surveys of both main communities in 1999 showed 80% support for entrenching economic and social rights to employment, health and housing, possibly linked to combating the high levels of deprivation in this part of the UK (NIHRC, 2001, p 84). However, there is no reference to trade union rights and a subsequent *Update* in 2004 (p 2) made it clear there was no intention to *guarantee* employment. The developments in Northern Ireland and parallel developments in Scotland where equality and human rights have been placed at the centre of the constitution through the 1998 Scotland Act demonstrate the increasing importance of rights-based discourses for social and economic policy across the UK.

Conclusion: the Equalities Review and possibilities for a politics of capabilities beyond workfare

This chapter has explored the possibilities for economic and social policy beyond workfare that can fully address the persistent patterns of exclusion and disadvantage identified through the SEQUAL research. Both Chapters Ten and Eleven have pointed to the partial success but diminishing returns associated with the mainstream work-first approach. They have identified the human capital approach as more promising, but particularly endorsed the stronger commitment to equalities issues within and outside the labour market, associated with a capabilities and human rights approach.

To conclude this chapter and the book as a whole we analyse two key areas of policy debate in the UK and Europe. First, the general discussion around capabilities that has emerged in European social policy circles that seek to map out an approach 'beyond Lisbon', to prevent economic and employment policy failures leading to a rightward shift towards more pronounced neoliberalism, as advocated by the 2004 Kok report. Second, as far as the UK is concerned, we sympathetically critique the framework developed by the Equalities Review (2007) to inform the work of the EHRC, which can potentially lead to a strengthening of efforts to focus on equalities issues in the post-Blair era.

The capabilities debate in Europe has emerged in response to the faltering effects of the European Employment Strategy (EES) to deliver the ambitious growth and employment targets of the Lisbon agenda, questioning the strong neoliberal emphasis on insertion into paid work, and the limited focus on inequalities issues. Salais (2005) has thus criticised Lisbon's excessive focus on job outcomes and advocated an alternative capabilities approach with development of appropriate objectives against which to evaluate policies. He argues that compulsory workfare is incompatible with this alternative approach. Dean et al (2005) have built on this to develop the capabilities framework into a 'thick' conception of needs and rights, arguing as a result for a 'life-first' rather than a 'work-first' approach, emphasising the importance of 'voice' and 'care'. The former would involve a shift from compulsion to more democratic and devolved employment services locally responsive to the articulated needs of disadvantaged communities. They see this as promoting a 'situated state' in contrast to the traditional 'technocratic' or neoliberal 'incentive-giving state'. This is strongly consistent with the need for genuine empowerment of communities that comes out of the SEQUAL research, although it tends to underplay the emphasis we have put on stronger demand-side intervention. Their emphasis on 'care' draws attention to the fact that much work, often carried out by women, occurs outside the sphere of paid employment. While access to the labour market can benefit women, it can also downgrade the social value of care. Williams (2001) has also highlighted these issues and argued for development of policies to recognise the validity of informal caring work and to empower both givers and receivers.

These debates often take place outside the rooms where policy decisions are made. The significance of the Equalities Review (2007) is in developing a conceptual framework and set of strategies based on capabilities and human rights to inform the practical policies of the EHRC. It clearly identifies the persistence of structural inequalities in gender, 'race', religion and belief, transgender, sexual orientation, age and disability, and highlights poverty and class-based economic inequality. The Review starts from a definition and vision of an equal society that borrows heavily from Sen with its emphasis on "real freedom and substantive opportunity to live in ways people value and would choose", in the light of people's "different needs, situations and goals" and a commitment to remove the barriers that prevent their realisation (Equality Review, 2007, p 126). From this it develops a set of capabilities drawn from international human rights frameworks covering both civil and political and economic, social and cultural rights, and from consultation with the general public and people at high risk of disadvantage. It proposes 10 capabilities for adults:

1   to be alive
2   to live in physical security
3   to be healthy
4   to be knowledgeable, to understand and reason, and to have the skills to participate in society
5   to enjoy a comfortable standard of living, with independence and security
6   to engage in productive and valued activities
7   to enjoy individual, family and social life
8   to participate in decision-making, have a voice and influence
9   of being and expressing yourself, and having self-respect
10   of knowing you will be protected and treated fairly by the law.
     (Equalities Review, 2007, pp 127-8)

These are further elaborated and translated into a set of 10 equality outcomes, for example, to be alive in terms of longevity, and so on, in order to identify equalities gaps, evaluate progress in closing them using a toolkit and an Equalities Scorecard to measure progress. This framework would cover gender, disability, religion and belief, transgender, sexual orientation, age, as well as 'socio-economic status'. There are many promising features of the Review for the work of the EHRC. For example, it proposes using public procurement in a concerted way and puts considerable emphasis on empowered disadvantaged communities, the need for which is endorsed by the SEQUAL research. As well as extending positive duties to all groups, it argues that the promised Single Equality Act should develop a group as well as an individual approach, but it does not go so far as to propose US-style 'affirmative action'.

Procurement apart, the Review does fall short in extending its perspective to the private and voluntary sectors and is silent on the question of whether economic, social and cultural rights should be constitutionally entrenched. These omissions mean that the framework described does not fully follow through the logic of the capabilities and human rights approach. While the Review advocates greater equality on economic, moral and social cohesion grounds, the emphasis is more on the first in asserting "equality is good for growth and prosperity" (Equalities Review, 2007, p 135). Sometimes this may be the case and a moral and political choice will need to be made. The Report critiques levelling down and proposes lifting those at the bottom, but without acknowledging that these are not mutually incompatible strategies.

Thus the tension already identified in Sen's work between humanism and capitalism is therefore faithfully reproduced in the Review. Nevertheless, despite the weaknesses and uncertainties about how policy will develop, the Equalities Review is undoubtedly a landmark publication that provides the essential starting point in the next stage for those who seek to campaign for labour market and welfare strategies that go beyond the workfare state and seek to realise equalities and human rights objectives.

References

Beresford, P. (2007) 'Wealth goes supernova', *Sunday Times*, 29 April (http://business.timesonline.co.uk/tol/business/specials/rich_list/article1708616.ece).

Blanden, J., Gregg, P. and Machin, S. (2005) *Intergenerational mobility in Europe and North America: A report supported by the Sutton Trust*, London: Centre for Economic Performance, London School of Economics and Political Science.

Brewer, M., Goodman, A., Alistair, M. and Sibieta, L. (2007) *Poverty and inequality in the UK: 2007*, IFS Briefing Note No 73, London: Institute for Fiscal Studies.

Clark, D.A. (2003) 'Conceptions and perceptions of human well-being: some evidence from South Africa', *Oxford Development Studies*, vol 31, no 2, pp 173-96.

Clark, D.A. (2005) *The capability approach: Its development, critiques and recent advances*, Manchester: Global Poverty Research Group, University of Manchester (www.gprg.org/pubs/workingpapers/pdfs/gprg-wps-032.pdf).

Clark, K. and Drinkwater, S. (2007) *Ethnic minorities in the labour market: Dynamics and diversity*, York: Joseph Rowntree Foundation.

Commission on Social Justice (2004) *Social justice: Strategies for national renewal*, London: Vintage.

Council of Europe (2004) *The Social Charter at a glance*, Strasbourg: Secretariat of the European Social Charter (http://conventions.coe.int/treaty/en/Treaties/Html/163.htm).

Craig, G., Wilkinson, M., Skrivankova, K. and McQuade, A. (2007) *Contemporary slavery in the UK: Overview and key issues*, York: Joseph Rowntree Foundation.

DCLG (Department of Communities and Local Government) (2007) *Towards a fairer future: Implementing the Women and Work Commission recommendations*, London: DCLG.

Dean, H., Bonvin, J.-M., Vielle, P. and Farvaque, N. (2005) 'Developing capabilities and rights in welfare-to-work policies', *European Societies*, vol 7, no 1, pp 3-26.

Dex, S. and Joshi, H. (2005) 'Mother's changing labour supply in Britain, the USA and Sweden', in R. Gomez-Salvador, A. Lamo, B. Petrongolo, M. Ward and E. Wasmer (eds) *Labour supply and incentives to work in Europe*, London: Edward Elgar, pp 115-50.

Donovan, P. (2006) 'Rethinking immigration', *The Guardian*, 18 August (http://commentisfree.guardian.co.uk/paul_donovan/2006/08/post_298.html).

Doyal, L. and Gough, I. (1991) *A theory of human need*, Basingstoke: Macmillan.

DTI (Department of Trade and Industry) (2006) *DTI News Release: Small Business Service statistical press release*, London: DTI (www.dtistats.net/smes/sme/smestats2005-ukspr.pdf).

ePolitix (2006) *Hutton backs 'crucial' pro-family policies*, London: ePolitix (www.epolitix.com).

Equalities Review (2007) *Fairness and freedom: The final report of the Equalities Review*, London: The Stationery Office.

Evans, M., Syrett, S. and Williams, C. (2006) *Informal economic activities and deprived neighbourhoods*, London: Department for Communities and Local Government.

Evans, P. (2002) 'Collective capabilities, culture, and Amartya Sen's "Development as freedom"', *Studies in Comparative International Development*, vol 32, no 2, pp 54-60.

Finn, D. and Simmonds, D. (2003) *Intermediate labour markets in Britain and an international review of transitional employment programmes*, London: Department for Work and Pensions.

Giddens, A. (1998) *The third way: The renewal of social democracy*, Cambridge: Polity.

Goos, M. and Manning, A. (2003) *Lousy and lovely jobs: The rising polarisation of work in Britain*, London: Centre for Economic Performance, London School of Economics and Political Science.

Gorz, A. (1999) *Reclaiming work: Beyond the wage-based society*, Cambridge: Polity.

Harker, L. (2006) *Delivering on child poverty: What would it take? A report for the Department of Work and Pensions*, Cm 6951, London: Department for Work and Pensions.

Hay, C. (2004) 'Credibility, competitiveness and the business cycle in "third way" political economy: a critical evaluation of economic policy in Britain since 1997', *New Political Economy*, vol 9, no 1, pp 39-56.

HM Treasury (2006) *Prosperity for all in the global economy – World class skills: final report* (Leitch Report), London: The Stationery Office.

Hoffman, D. and Rowe, J. (2006) *Human rights in the UK: An introduction to the Human Rights Act 1998* (2nd edn), Harlow, Essex: Pearson Education.

Hollingshead, I. (2006) 'Whatever happened to ... the 48-hour week', *The Guardian*, 28 January.

Hudson, M. (2006) *The hidden 1 in 5: Winning a fairer deal for Britain's vulnerable workers*, London: Trades Union Congress.

Ibrahim, S.S. (2006) 'From individual to collective capabilities: the capability approach as a conceptual framework for self-help', *Journal of Human Development*, vol 7, no 3, pp 397-416.

I-UK (2007) *Huge bonuses for city workers* (www.i-uk.com).

Johnson, N. (2004) 'The Human Rights Act 1998: a bridge between citizenship and justice?', *Social Policy and Society*, vol 3, no 2, pp 113-21.

Katungi, D., Neale, E. and Barbour, A. (2006) *People in low-paid informal work: 'Need not greed'*, York: Joseph Rowntree Foundation.

Klug, F. (2005) 'Human rights: above politics or a creature of politics?', *Policy & Politics*, vol 33, no 1, pp 3-14.

Kochan, T., Bezrukova, K. and Ely, R. et al (2003) 'The effects of business performance: report of the Diversity Research Network', *Human Resource Management*, vol 42, no 1, pp 3-21.

Knell, J., Oalkey, K. and O'Leary, D. (2007) *Confronting the skills paradox*, London: Demos.

Lawson, N. (2006) 'The nation of shoppers needs to talk about class', *The Guardian*, 19 April (www.guardian.co.uk/commentisfree/story/0,,1756367,00.html).

Levitas, R. (2001) 'Against work: a utopian incursion to social policy', *Critical Social Policy*, vol 21, no 4, pp 449-65.

Lloyd, C. and Payne, J. (2002) 'On "the political economy of skill": assessing the possibilities for a viable high skills project in the UK', *New Political Economy*, vol 7, no 3, pp 367-95.

McLaughlin, E. (2007) 'From negative to positive equality duties: the development and constitutionalisation of equality provisions in the UK', *Social Policy and Society*, vol 6, no 1, pp 111-21.

Monbiot, G. (2006) *Heat: How to stop the planet burning*, London: Allen Lane.

NGH (National Group on Homeworking) (2006) *Equal rights equals employment rights*, Leeds: NGH Ltd (www.ngh.org.uk).

NIHRC (Northern Ireland Human Rights Commission) (2001) *Making a Bill of Rights for Northern Ireland: A consultation by the NIHRC*, Belfast: NIHRC (www.borini.info/uploads/documents/BoR_consultation.pdf).

Nolan, P. (2004) 'The changing world of work', *Journal for Health Services Research and Policy*, vol 9, no 1, Supplement 1, pp 3-9.

Nussbaum, M.C. (2003) 'Capabilities as fundamental entitlement: Sen and social justice', *Feminist Economics*, vol 9, nos 2-3, pp 33-59.

ONS (Office for National Statistics) (2006) *Society: Share of the wealth*, London: ONS (www.statistics.gov.uk/cci/nugget.asp?id=2).

ONS (2007) *Income inequality: Rise in inequality in 2005/06*, London: ONS (www.statistics.gov.uk/cci/nugget.asp?id=332).

Orton, M. and Ratcliffe, P. (2005) 'New Labour ambiguity, or neo-liberal consistency? The debate about racial inequality in employment and the use of contract compliance', *Journal of Social Policy*, vol 34, no 2, pp 255-72.

Palmer, G., MacInnes, T. and Kenway, P. (2006) *Monitoring poverty and social exclusion*, York: Joseph Rowntree Foundation.

Parliamentary Joint Committee on Human Rights (2004) *The International Covenant on economic, social and cultural rights: Twenty-first report of Session 2003-04*, London: The Stationery Office.

Peck, J. and Theodore, N. (2000) 'Beyond "Employability"', *Cambridge Journal of Economics*, vol 24, no 6, pp 729-49.

Platt, L. (2005) *Migration and social mobility: The life chances of Britain's ethnic minority communities*, York: Joseph Rowntree Foundation.

Roth, B.R. (2004) 'Retrieving Marx for the human rights project', *Leiden Journal of International Law*, vol 17, no 1, pp 31-66.

Ruxton, S. and Karim, R. (2001) *Beyond civil rights: Developing economic, social and cultural rights in the UK*, Oxford: Oxfam GB in association with JUSTICE.

Salais, R. (2005) 'Incorporating the capability approach into social and employment policies', in R. Salais and R. Villeneuve (eds) *Europe and the politics of capabilities*, Cambridge: Cambridge University Press, pp 283-300.

Salway, S., Platt, L., Chowbey, P., Harriss, K. and Bayliss, E. (2007) *Long-term ill health, poverty and ethnicity*, York: Joseph Rowntree Foundation.

Sen, A. (1999) *Development as freedom*, Oxford: Oxford University Press.

Smith, P. and Morton, G. (2006) 'Nine years of New Labour: neoliberalism and workers' rights', *British Journal of Industrial Relations*, vol 44, no 3, pp 401-20.

T&G News (2007) 'Trade unions say fight for workers' rights go on', London: Transport and General Workers Union, 2 March (www. tgwu.org.uk).

Temko, N. (2007) 'Lib Dems plan wealth tax on £1 million homes', *The Guardian*, 4 March (http://money.guardian.co.uk/tax/story/0,,2026199,00.html).

TUC (Trades Union Congress) (2006b) *Trade Union Freedom Bill: Explanatory notes*, London: TUC.

Williams, F. (2001) 'In and beyond New Labour: towards a new political ethics of care', *Critical Social Policy*, vol 21, no 4, pp 467-93.

Wills, J. (2004) 'The East London Communities Organisation (TELCO) living wage campaign', in W. Brown, G. Healy, E. Heery and P. Taylor (eds) *The future of worker representation*, Oxford: Oxford University Press, pp 264-82.

Vizard, P. (2006) *Briefing note: The HDCA approach and human rights*, Cambridge, MA: Human Development and Capability Association (www.capabilityapproach.com/pubs/HumanRights100306.pdf).

Index